Letters

MW01616391

Carlos Valenzuela

Dedication

It takes a village to write a book. Thank you, John Biggers, screenwriter, who first saw merit in young Carlos's story. Tatay, my eternal childhood bestie, and my blog followers who keep the candle lit.

Acknowledgment

To the divergent who embrace their essence and those who love them.

About the Author

Carlos Valenzuela is a consultant for the professional beauty industry with a master's in international management. Carlos grew up along the border city of Agua Prieta, Sonora, with Douglas, Arizona. He traveled worldwide as a spokesperson and trainer for major beauty brands and authored numerous educational beauty training programs. His technical and personal development philosophy continues to influence thousands of salon professionals everywhere. A frequent presenter at major beauty events and on his online website www.carlos-valenzuela.com, he is a regular contributor to Modern Salon on professional and personal development and The Stylist News on personal money management. Letters to Young Carlos, a novella about a gay boy growing up along the US-Mexico border in the 1960s, is his first novel.

Preface

One cannot suppress past lives because they no longer fit in the present. Nothing can erase the memories of my days growing up on the border. Sheer white curtains billowing free from an open window ushering the smell of first raindrops on parched soil, a local orchestra playing on a summer night as I dance around the kiosk at the Plaza Azueta, the hugs, and tears at the stroke of midnight on New Year's Eve in the old Casino de Agua Prieta dance hall. Unforgettable.

The tall pine tree, whose thick trunk I leaned against for my Papa to measure my height, is no longer there, but I still see the tree with my mind's eye. I still feel my father's love reassuring me I am taller than I was two days ago. My Mama lit the same tree with tiny blue lights in December to the beat of my anxious young heart. The echo of her sweet laughter will forever live in my memory. Still today, my spirits lift, sensing a woman's joy.

We love to relive the moment. Memories eternalize experiences and rejuvenate the spirit, if only momentarily, just like delicate morning dew refreshes tender green and vanishes with the light of day.

Oh, and the eternal bond of friendship. How is it that the universe provides that special someone just when the world seems darkest? When I felt I shared everything and nothing with everyone, I learned to love the person. Not because they were perfect, but by seeing their perfection in my life. Some hearts feel so familiar. As if they somehow knew each other before they met. I am a collection of these strangers' love. My heart is a rich repository of all the ways I've loved and been loved.

A divergent heart subsisting on lukewarm understanding knows that stealth indifference, far more bewildering than outright rejection, is incompatible with belonging. I identified early on with silent voices at odds with imposed expectations, starting when society judged my existence as an aberration. "Why me?" remains a mystery, but one where resiliency of the human spirit triumphs. As elder Carlos says, "It's painful to learn love doesn't come from those given to you but from those you must find along the way."

My life is blessed but not remarkable enough to merit publication. Letters to Young Carlos is a fictional novella and not my story. The characters are from my imagination or borrowed from those I've met along the way.

Although fictional and set in the 1960s, young Carlos's bildungsroman resonates with people, gay or straight, who walk to the beat of their own drum.

I love young Carlos because he seeks to understand life's most challenging mystery: to love oneself and others and be loved in return.

Contents

Page Left Blank Intentionally

Chapter 1: The Aroma of Passion

He escaped from kindergarten, wearing only his underwear. Ashamed and embarrassed, he ran up the driveway towards the inner safety of his home. He passed his Papa getting into his truck, who averted his gaze with embarrassment. Popi greeted him with excitement, but upon sensing something wrong, he lowered his head and tail. Crying out, he rounded the house's corner and headed towards the back door where his Mama would stand at the kitchen sink. He yelled her name, but she could not hear him. He screamed for help louder this time. But still, nobody listened to his cries for help. Finally, he rushed up to his mother and buried his face in the folds of her skirt in deep sobs.

Carlos Casavantes opened his eyes while panting, and his heart throbbing. He was relieved when he realized that he was still in bed at the Casa Alegre Nursing Home. No matter how many times he had that dream, he always broke into a sweat. He got out of bed and looked around the room, like many mornings when he first woke up. His scant belongings were proof of a life of loving and living reduced to a bed, a narrow closet, a chest of drawers, and a lone window. He spent hours looking out the window and to the partial view of a California Chinese elm. Its hanging colors and rounded, multi-branched crown atop and thick trunk, which grew in girth with age, helped him keep track of the passage of time.

Pulling a well-worn navy-blue robe from a hanger, he sniffed its collar before putting it on as he often did. Despite the laundering, it kept the slightest scent of Jesse, the love of his life. It smelled of the many times they sat side by side, their hearts racing, their eyes momentarily meeting, forbidden from showing their love for one another. Those moments had an aroma of passion he now sought to retrieve from the worn robe.

He sighed and pulled his arms through the wide sleeves. Did he sense a fragrance, or was it a longing for moments in the past? Suppose life is all about remembering past moments. If so, he will stay away from the ones that hurt most—those impossible ones, nostalgia for what never was, and a desire for what could have been. Those can pierce right through an older man's heart.

The solitude of his life wasn't new. He slipped into invisibility once before. At least this time, he wouldn't need the painful adjustment period. He knew what it felt like to walk into a room full of cheerful people and nobody looking up. He was there before, at an innocent young age and with much fewer defenses.

After he washed up, he sat in his comfortable chair to gaze at the elm tree outside the window. The leaves were now a blend of green and yellow, announcing the fall season and the holidays. The nursing home celebrations only reminded him of Christmas on the border and how his childish heart's innocence magnified the good while washing out the bad.

If life is now about remembering the past, he will document the memories that made him smile. One day he may not recall any memories and have to make them up just to stay alive. Before that happened and his macular degeneration erased the words from his pages, he would write down as many memories as possible. The lessons learned from crossing the river of life might help others stay afloat if they knew where the rocks are. Yes, that's what he would do.

Chapter 2: The Invisible Handicap

Nurse Laila carried a meal tray along the Casa Alegre retirement home hallway and made a quick turn into room #303. There, she saw elder Carlos sitting in his pajamas and robe by a small table with a writing tablet and pen in hand.

Seeing Carlos at his table, Nurse Laila attempted to rouse him and catch his attention, "How're you doing today, Mr. Carlos. Feeling good?" She asked him.

Carlos did not look up from his writing, so Nurse Laila placed the food tray on a table close to him and stood awaiting a reply.

"You hungry today, Mr. Carlos? Look, I brought you some nice chicken soup and your favorite Hershey Chocolate bar with almonds. I know you like those almonds."

Carlos wearily looked at the food tray with a faint smile and said, "Chicken soup, chocolate bar? It all tastes the same now."

"Oh, come on! You know you love your Hershey's chocolate almond bar. Besides, your taste buds change as you get a little older. Some folks here can't tell hot from cold, sweet from salty. It's all the same to them."

Carlos silently picked up his pen to return to his writing. Nurse Laila's responsibility was to ensure the elderly residents nourished themselves to avoid debilitation, and Carlos was not cooperating. She tried coming in from a different angle.

"Are you writing another one of your letters?" She asked curiously.

But Carlos kept writing. Nurse Laila's voice grew more insistent, "Who's it for? Are you going to let me read this one too?" Carlos didn't respond. "Okay, you got me, Mr. Carlos. What's this letter about? At least give me a clue."

"It's about becoming," he answered, taking off his reading glasses.

Nurse Laila felt she was making progress and asked, "Becoming? Becoming what? Famous, old, a struggling writer? That's one strange letter, Mr. Carlos."

Nurse Laila liked her job and was good at it. She emanated a desire to share confidences from anyone she met. She cared for the elderly with commendable humanity. Nobody knew much about her life outside the nursing home. She would mention her teenage son, Roy, occasionally, but never a husband or father of her son. She emerged unscathed through the tough times she might have endured. Nurse Laila was a very private person.

"It's about living with an invisible handicap," replied Carlos.

She saw an opening and took it, "Now, have a taste of my soup and talk to me about how anyone can have an invisible handicap? You mean to tell me someone can have an invisible wheelchair, a cane, or a crutch?" She asked.

Carlos knew the game she was playing and obligingly picked up his spoon. "It's invisible because you feel you have everything and nothing in common with the world, and there's this big secret that if you tell, everyone will pass you up." He said. The only weakness Nurse Laila ever displayed was a fondness for sweets, attested by a few extra pounds around her midriff. If she worried, she never betrayed her cheerful countenance. Right now, getting Carlos to eat his lunch was the only thing on her mind.

"Pass you up? How would you know about being passed up? Let me tell you. I never know who's going to say hello or pass me up next every day.

Some liked me fine yesterday, but not today. How's that soup working out for you?"

"But Laila, you can't hide your Blackness. Every day you leave home, you must be Black. Some folks hide who they really are. They live a lie. It's tough to feel honest or be good at anything when you keep who you are a secret in your heart."

"Are you saying you and I have something in common? I know everyone wants to get rid of something, Mr. Carlos. Like a rash, a husband, or a nasty reputation. Have your soup, eat your chocolate, and write your letter. I'll read it when you're done, and we'll go from there."

Nurse Laila checked her wristwatch. She realized she spent too much time with elder Carlos and started making her way to the door. "Let me know when you finish that soup and write that letter. I want to know more about this invisible handicap."

"Thanks for the chocolate bar, Laila."

Nurse Laila moved like a cat. She tiptoed and closed the door to elder Carlos's room without a sound and disappeared. Carlos put his food tray to the side and returned to his writing.

Dear Young Carlos,

It's okay to be different. It's okay not to be like everyone else. You come from a world nobody yet understands. It's painful to learn love doesn't come from those given to you but from those you must find along the way.

You will clash with the righteous, the bully, and the whisperer. Your mere presence shakes the foundation of the narrow sliver of happiness some have managed to carve out for themselves.

Try not to take things personally. You are perfect just the way you are. Nothing others do or say is because of you but a projection of their reality.

To be free, you will need to leave behind many things you now love. This will bring you great sadness. Stay strong. Trust your heart because, despite the odds, you win. Eventually, you will understand why you are who you had to be—your life plants seeds for a better tomorrow for those who will come after you.

You will never forget those who touched your heart. Regardless if they healed or broke it, and you will forgive them all. Most of all, you will forgive yourself.

Remember, I love you, and I will never abandon you.

Your Elder Self.

Chapter 3: The Awakening

Carlitos, age six, lies in his bed awake. He was awoken by the loud voices coming from the kitchen.

"I never wanted to marry you. It was my mother who wanted you for a daughter. I never loved you and never will," Facundo yelled, pounding a kitchen table.

"Really?" replied Blanca, "And my mother said, 'I know you don't love him. You will learn to love him.' Well, you haven't made it easy." She replied in the same manner.

The Casavantes household was usually up by six in the morning. It was a habit from the days of living on the ranch when an early start cut down on the hours working under a scorching sun. Carlitos' parents, Facundo and Blanca, lived on the ranch when they first married. Once his older sister Bonita and he were born, the family moved to the border town of Agua Prieta with Douglas, Arizona.

Los Laureles Ranch was a rural settlement dating from the 1880s. It was mainly used for breeding Hereford cattle. The rustic home offered few modern conveniences for a young family—a wood-burning stove, kerosene lamps, an outhouse, no indoor plumbing, and no refrigerator. The winters were long, followed by intense summer heat. The men needed to be macho-tough to withstand rural living challenges and provide for their devoted women—the women reciprocated by caring for the man, home, and children. The children were expected to show an inclination for the elder's footsteps from an early age. Blanca was ambitious and wanted a better life for herself and her children. She sought escape from Los Laureles and convinced Facundo to move them to the border for their children's education. The new surroundings only stressed the differences in the couple's values and escalated their conflict.

On this particular morning, Carlitos stared at the ceiling, listening to the angry voices. His father always seemed to pick the early morning when everyone was asleep to fight with his mother. Maybe he hoped his actions might go unnoticed at that early hour. Carlitos had seen his mother cry once after the morning arguments, and he didn't want ever to see her cry again. He sighed as he quickly got out of bed and made his way past a well-furnished living room toward the kitchen as the voices escalated.

"You certainly don't mind my money, do you? You have no problem spending it!"

"I spend money on the children. Your children. They will have everything you and I never got and much more if I have to drain the last peso from your wallet."

"Oh yeah? And you know what will happen to you then?" He asked venomously.

Carlitos burst through the kitchen door and stood, arms outstretched in front of Blanca, preventing Facundo from striking a blow. "Don't hurt my Mama. Don't make her cry. You're scaring me," cried Carlitos with tears starting to stream down his face.

Facundo's rage-filled eyes locked on Carlitos, but the sight of the small boy crying for his mother disarmed him. He picked up Carlitos and held him suspended in the air for a few seconds. "Put him down!" yelled Blanca. After a few tense moments, Facundo brought Carlitos down and stormed out, muttering obscenities under his breath and slamming the kitchen door behind him, making Carlitos shudder. Blanca composed herself, stooped down to his height, and cradled him by his shoulders. "I'm here, little one. Don't be frightened," said Blanca, "We grown-ups sometimes speak very loudly, don't we? I'm sorry we woke you up to see this. Thank you for coming to my rescue. You are my hero." She kissed his cheek and softly brushed his brown hair with her hand, and said, "Look at the time! Quick, put on your altar boy tunic, or we'll be late for the children's mass."

Blanca was an attractive woman in her early forties from a nearby mining town. Her father, the son of a Welsh immigrant, worked in the town's copper mine until his untimely death. She had several brothers and sisters, but she was her father's favorite. It was a preference that her mother thoroughly resented. With her father gone, Blanca's upbringing became vengeful and strict. Her widow-mother woke her daily before dawn to begin the household chores. Her only outlet was the Church, never an outing or event.

It was customary to have several children and select one to remain single to care for the aging parents. Blanca feared she was the chosen one due to her strict upbringing and limited social contact. She met Facundo when she served lunch for him and his parents on a rare visit to Blanca's mother. She quickly sized him up as a man who could love any woman and be her escape from home. Facundo was an easy lure. He was allowed to visit and eventually propose to Blanca because of his considerable influence and wealth. Her mother never showed a sign of joy nor well-wishes for her marriage, despite Facundo bringing her expensive perfumery, veils, and sweets during his chaperoned Saturday night visits to Blanca. That is how Carlitos' parents met and set out to form a family. However, their fairytale was short-lived as reality caught up to them. Their opposing values made raising a family a constant source of escalating conflict and abuse. In time, their parenting and marital responsibilities proved to be bigger than themselves.

Minutes later, Carlitos, dressed in a red altar boy tunic, sat in the passenger seat of a brand new '52 Chevrolet Bel Air with his older sister Bonita in the back seat. Facundo walked up the driveway and knocked on the car window. As Carlitos rolled down the window, Facundo pulled out a bill from his front pocket and held it in the air for Carlitos to see.

"Here, so you can go to the Sunday movies and invite one of your little friends."

"Gracias, Papa," said Carlitos. Facundo handed him the money and added, "You know you are my little man, right? You love your Papa, don't you?" Carlitos stared at Facundo, unsure of the sudden change in his mood, "As soon as you get a little older, you will come to the ranch and learn to be a cowboy just like me."

Blanca opened the car door and got in the driver's seat. Without a word, she backed up the car from the driveway. She drove onto Calle Primera in Our Lady of Guadalupe Church's direction. The town's unpaved streets were either rivers of mud in the rainy season or dust clouds in the dry season. Facundo stood in the dust cloud left behind by Blanca and watched the family drive away.

It was a short drive to Our Lady of Guadalupe Church. Carlitos sat in silence and sporadically raised his head to check their travel progress. As they neared the Church, he asked Blanca, "Do I have to go to the ranch with Papa?"

Blanca's mind seemed distant as she said, "Only if you want to. If you don't want to, you can do something else."

"I don't want to be a cowboy. I want to be a movie star and sing and dance like Fred Astaire."

"Of course, you do. Of course, you do," said Blanca looking around for a parking space, "We'll talk about it after mass, alright?"

"Can I ask Miguelito to go to the movies with me? Papa gave me five pesos. Please, can I? Please?"

"After mass, Carlos."

Chapter 4: The Altar Boy

The church bells were ringing as Blanca parked the family car. The bells rang at three different times before the start of services alerting the faithful to make their way to the Church as mass was about to begin.

Carlitos took his place with the altar boys at the Church's atrium and waited for the last bell to lead a procession down the aisle to the main altar. Every Sunday, his spot was at the start of the lineup, holding a tall crucifix. Next to him was his friend, Miguelito, carrying a large missal. Carlos and Miguelito's diminutive figure, the smallest of altar boys performing solemn religious duties, always attracted the churchgoers' admiration and praise.

With the third bell and the first organ notes, Padre Sancho and the altar boys began walking down the Church aisle. The priest alternated his blessing from side to side as he walked toward the altar. Blanca and Bonita watched Carlitos walk by as the choir and congregation sang, *"Ven Corazon Mio."*

Padre Sancho's ministry packed more punch than any politician or local personality. The faithful, predominantly women, attended the Church, covering their hair as it was a symbol of beauty and lust. They wore high buttoned-up collars, long-sleeved blouses, and long skirts. The Padre enjoyed the well-earned reputation of stopping mid-service and asking any lady to excuse herself from Church and return with more appropriate clothing.

When the procession finally arrived at the main altar, the Padre solemnly bowed, picked up a handheld microphone, and turned to the congregation, "The Lord be with you."

"And with your spirit," the people replied in unison.

"Today is the first Sunday of the month," Padre Sancho announced, "There will be a special collection for the poor. We also pray for the eternal rest of Guadalupe Araiza. May her soul rest in peace."

"And may perpetual light shine upon her," the faithful answered.

"My children, remember, that catechism is today at eleven. And may I remind you again, children, you can only see movies rated "A" by the Legion of Decency. Any movie rated B, C, or Z is a mortal sin to watch," he added.

Carlitos, standing to Padre Sancho's right, leaned the tall crucifix to the side to get a glance of Miguelito, who shrugged his shoulders and grinned. The Padre continued, "Children if you follow the laws of the Church, you will be good Christians, marry and raise the good children God sends you. If you sin and suddenly die without confessing your sins, you will burn in the fires of hell forever." Carlitos' eyes opened wide as he shot another look at Miguelito, who scratched his head and rolled his eyes.

After mass, Carlitos and Miguelito tossed their tunics into a sacristy closet. They ran down the empty Church to the atrium. They stopped in front of a bulletin board where a white sheet read, "Movie Classifications," in large letters.

"Oh, no! The movie *Los Marcianos Llegaron Ya* (The Martians Have Landed) is a C-1. We can't see it!" said Carlitos.

Miguelito stared at the bulletin notice, "That's because this lady comes out dancing and shows all her legs. I mean, all her legs, all the way up!"

"Really? There's dancing?" Carlitos asked, "You want to sneak in anyways? I've got five pesos for the tickets. We'll even have enough for popcorn."

"Que padre! Let's go." Miguelito exclaimed excitedly.

"I'll meet you outside the Cinema Alhambra at one o'clock. I've got to go now, though. Mama is waiting for me in the car."

"Cinema Alhambra?" whined Miguelito, "Are you crazy? Doña Laura sells the tickets there. She'll tell Padre Sancho and call my mom and your mom."

Carlitos and Miguelito remained pensive for a minute. "I know," said Carlitos, "I'll disguise myself. I'm good at dressing up, and Doña Laura will never recognize me. I will go up to her in disguise and ask for two tickets in a really deep voice, and then we'll run inside."

Carlitos and Miguelito shook hands and laughed.

Cinema Alhambra was the only movie house in Agua Prieta and a popular Sunday outing. The pricier *Luneta* seats on the main floor were more comfortable than the bargain *Galeria* seats overlooking *Luneta* that were concrete bleachers and a continuous source of pranks and misbehavior.

The *Galeria* folks accompanied the on-screen drama with foot-stomping for the good guys, kissing sounds for idol Enrique Guzman and pretty Angelica Maria, and warning whistles when the monster was sneaking up anyone. They booed the bad guys every moment on screen. But you could hear a pin drop in Tizoc when famous Pedro Infante says to beautiful Maria Felix, "I love you more than my eyes, but I love my eyes more because they see you."

Carlitos arrived at the Cinema Alhambra's lobby wearing Facundo's sunglasses, an oversized sports coat in the midday heat, and a baseball cap. Believing himself to be well-disguised, he approached the ticket booth as Miguelito ducked out of the ticket seller's view. Doña Laura, famous for her over-powdered white face, red hot lips, and rhinestone eyeglasses, sat in the ticket booth looking bored and filing her nails.

Carlitos approached the ticket window confidently, but Doña Laura instantly pegged him.

"Carlitos, what brings you here?" she asked.

"Huh? Err... *Buenas tardes,* Doña Laura. Oh, you know, just buying two tickets for my parents."

"Really? And where are they? I don't see them," she said suspiciously.

"Err... They are parking the car."

"Really? I'll give them their tickets when they get here," she shrugged.

"Oh, no, Doña Laura. You don't want to do that. That's going to make Papa very angry, and he is likely to yell at you really loudly. Have you ever seen him when he's angry?" He said with wide eyes.

Carlitos grinned, held out his five pesos, and waited. Doña Laura reluctantly handed him two tickets and his change. "*Gracias,* Doña Laura. Bye-bye for now!"

Carlitos ran past the Cinema Alhambra's wide front doors with Miguelito following behind, and they disappeared into the theater's darkness. Miguelito quickly spotted two good seats, and they sat patiently, waiting for the young man walking the aisles selling popcorn. The popcorn salesman stretched out the word *"esquite"* to alert all he was approaching, "*Essssquite, essssquite."*

They shared a bag of popcorn fixated on the musical number as Evangelina Elizondo danced and sang, "*Los Marcianos Llegaron Ya,*" with la Vitola and Resortes. The Galeria people whistled at Evangelina Elizondo, laughed at la Vitola, and cheered for Resortes.

The darkness of the theater was a golden opportunity to act out impulsively. Couples embraced and kissed passionately with an occasional whiff of a lunch fart floating through the air. A woman silenced her companion, who repeatedly tried to guess the next scene in a loud voice. A lonesome man slowly inched his hand to touch the hand of the pretty woman sitting one seat away from him, but she pulled away in disgust. The Galeria fans tossed items over the balcony, aiming for a perfect landing on carefully coiffed heads below. On-screen, Evangelina Elizondo danced, showing off her beautiful legs to foot-stomping loud whistles from the Galeria. Miguelito yelled out, "*Hijole,* look at those legs!"

Chapter 5: Tulio and The Saturday Morning Playhouse

Boys on bicycles delivered the Douglas Daily Dispatch to the few English-speaking homes in Agua Prieta. Bikes lined up after school outside the Dispatch offices, picking up the afternoon paper to deliver in Douglas and Agua Prieta. The boys folded the paper into a tight, flat square to toss it like a frisbee and hopefully land near the front door.

Tulio, the youngest of paperboys, rode his bike on Calle Primera's sidewalks, tossing newspapers as he passed by. He turned into Carlitos' driveway and rang the front doorbell. Blanca came to the door as Tulio stood on his bike panting with one foot on the bike pedal.

"Buenas tardes, Doña Blanca."

"Hola, Tulio," she said, thinking she was about to hear a pitch for a subscription, she added, "*Lo siento*, but we don't take the Dispatch because, as you know, nobody here speaks English. Would you like a glass of water or a soda instead?" offered Blanca.

"Oh, no, Doña Blanca, I came to ask if Carlitos can come and play theatre at my house on Saturday?" Carlitos carefully snuck up and stood listening behind Blanca's wide skirt out of Tulio's sight.

"I suppose so," Blanca answered, "I've never heard of that game. How do you play it?"

"We play records, sing, and dance, pretending we are the ones singing the song, and the neighborhood kids come and watch. It's like a real theatre. My mom says it's okay."

Carlitos' eyes widened with excitement, and he yanked on Blanca's skirt from behind. Feeling the tug on her dress, Blanca answered, "I...I think it will be alright." He poked his head out from behind Blanca for a quick look at Tulio as he peddled away. Tulio laughed when he realized Carlitos was listening all along and gave him an approving wink. "Okay, Carlitos. See you Saturday morning. Don't be late, *hasta luego.*"

Tulio was a year older than Carlitos and the son of an American mother and Mexican father. They knew the Casavantes family well. Tulio spoke English fluently. His family and upbringing were more liberal and better adapted to American ways than the Casavantes.

Saturday morning, Carlitos, dressed in his Sunday best, per Blanca's instructions, walked up Tulio's pathway to the front door and knocked. The housekeeper opened the door and said, "They are all down in the basement. Go ahead."

Carlitos took the stairs to the basement as a children's song, "Zippy Dee Doo Dah," played loudly. As he entered the room, Tulio lip-synced and danced to the music on a makeshift stage, wearing a cape, top hat, and stage makeup. Younger children sat on boxes and the floor in front of the stage, watching him perform. Tulio stopped his performance as he saw young Carlos walk into the room. "*Hola,* Carlitos. Do you want to sing a song? Which one would you like to sing?"

Carlitos answered, "I...I don't know. I can't sing."

"Yes, you can. Here, let's sing and dance together." Tulio picked up a derby hat and awkwardly plopped it on top of Carlitos' head. Then stood back and observed, "Hm, you're going to need some makeup."

Tulio patted powder on the face of his new friend with a large puff. Next, he dabbed a bit of rouge. "This will bring out your features for the stage," he said. "Now, slightly open up so I can put some lipstick right in the center of your lips." He checked the look one last time, "There, now you look like a real movie star." Carlitos was in a daze, loving it.

Tulio placed the needle at the start of the "Zippy Dee Doo Dah" record and, as the song started, began dancing to music, keeping his eyes fixed on Carlitos. After a few dance moves, he extended his arm. He took Carlitos' hand, leading him onto the stage with slow, deliberate movements. After a few moves, Tulio upped the performance and made a majestic turn, then pointed to Carlitos to do the same. The children in the audience cheered as he awkwardly imitated the gestures. Carlitos continued dancing, imitating Tulio until the song ended, "This is fun, Tulio!"

"See, you're good! Let's do another one. You want to?!"

"I can do this forever!" Carlitos cheered as they locked arms and celebrated their newfound connection, jumping up and down with joy.

Dear Young Carlos,

You found a real friend. One who hears the song in your heart and will sing it back if you forget. One with whom you can stand naked and bare your soul without shame. A real friend is a master teacher. Tulio will teach you that friendship is defending your friend's happiness, no matter what it is. Always know what a friend needs and be there for them.

Many friends will say they feel your pain, but only the sincerest heart feels your joy. There's no friend ever like the one that knows you since you were a child. Love him like a brother. Miles may separate you, but everything will always remain the same. This is no ordinary friendship.

Your Elder Self.

Chapter 6: First Day of School

Blanca learned to cook from an early age without the convenience of a grocery store. In her childhood home, every ingredient came directly from the source. Coffee was home roasted and ground, as were all spices. She knew how to quarter a butchered animal into prime cuts. Now, with a Safeway just five minutes across the border, she upped her game and created meals in minutes. Her cooking skills evolved into a hybrid version of northern Mexico specialties with newly discovered American conveniences. Blanca became a fantastic cook.

At breakfast, Facundo scooped his *chorizo con huevos* with a freshly made flour tortilla into his mouth. He studied Carlitos for a few seconds and muttered, "Carlos has to go to school here in Agua Prieta, not in Douglas. Those *gringo* nuns turn boys into sissies. He needs to learn to saddle up and ride bareback and learn what real men do."

Children from upper-class families in Agua Prieta often attended Loretto School on the Douglas, Arizona, side of the border. Dominican nuns from Michigan, who spoke no Spanish, practiced a more liberal version of Catholicism, often clashing with Padre Sancho's more "traditional" views. Attending Loretto would be a challenge for Carlitos, who spoke no English. Still, Blanca wanted him to have a Catholic education, so she pushed Loretto. "He needs to learn English," she said.

"Papa, all the kids we know go to that school. Everyone!" said Bonita, who was entering her teens and growing up to become a beautiful woman. Like most women she knew, her goal was to marry her boyfriend Luis, have children, and live happily ever after. She wouldn't allow anything like the way Facundo treated her mother. Bonita often disagreed with her father and always stood up for herself.

"I don't care who goes where. Those kids aren't the son of Facundo Casavantes," he said with a stern look at Bonita.

Undeterred, she responded, "Do that, and he'll hate you for it. If that's what you want, go ahead."

"He'll go to the ranch when he's a little older. Right now, he needs schooling on the American side," Blanca added, starting to pick up the breakfast dishes.

Thinking he would get the last word, Facundo began getting up from the table, saying, "He has to learn to act like a real Mexican man, with machismo and dignity."

Blanca forcefully turned on the sink faucet with a big splash, "You want him to be macho, and I want him to be smart."

Carlitos waited for a moment of silence before chiming in, "I'm going to be a movie star. That's what I am going to be."

"*Silencio!* You will be no such thing," yelled Facundo, "You will work your father's ranch, marry, and have a family like me."

Blanca came to the rescue, "Stop yelling, Facundo. It's a child's fantasy. You just confuse him. You confuse me!" Facundo finally threw down his napkin and left the kitchen.

Carlitos lowered his head and stared at the floor. Blanca walked away from the kitchen sink and came by his side. She gently picked up his head by the chin. "We'll talk about movie stars later. For now, you need to go to the American school with your friend Tulio."

"But, Mama, how will I understand what they say? I don't speak English," he asked.

"Tulio speaks English. He will help you. I already spoke to his mother," said Blanca, "Besides, you need to speak good English to be a movie star, don't you?"

Carlitos beamed.

Weeks later, Bonita dropped Carlitos off at Loretto School's front entrance. He ran and quickly found Tulio to follow in his footsteps. Bonita was protective of young Carlos ever since she looked after him all by herself when she was a child. Blanca taught her to prepare his baby food, feed him, and change his diapers. She was eight years older, leading her to believe that Carlitos' birth was probably unplanned.

A nun rang a handbell, signaling the start of classes. Children in blue and white uniforms lined up by grade, awaiting their respective nun to lead them to their classroom. Bonita sat in the car and kept an eye on Carlitos until she saw a young nun take him and Tulio by the hand and guide them inside the school.

Carlitos' desk was in the center of the classroom, surrounded by blonde and blue-eyed children. Tulio sat directly behind him. The Sister gave instructions in English, and Carlitos turned to Tulio, shrugging his shoulders. Tulio, whispering in Spanish, said, "She's saying you may not speak in Spanish. Only English is allowed."

Panic settled into Carlitos' heart, "What?" He needed the restroom and didn't know how to communicate it to the nun. He rubbed his knees together, trying to subdue the urge. Finally, he got up to find the bathroom, but the Sister, unaware of his need, returned him to his desk. Not able to hold on any longer, he let go and peed in his pants. The students pointed at him and broke out in laughter. Carlitos ran out of the classroom. Tulio followed, saying, "Carlos, wait!"

He stopped at the curb, waiting to cross the street as Tulio caught up with him, "Hey, you want me to take you home?" Carlitos kept his head down and nodded in agreement.

"I'm never coming back here," he uttered under his breath.

Tulio did not like what he heard, "Hey, Carlitos. Yesterday, Roberta Smith? The girl with the red hair? Yeah, yesterday she took a big shit in her panties. And Pedro, the chubby kid that keeps following us around? He pissed in his pants, too. Everyone is shitting themselves all over the place."

Carlitos kept his head lowered in silence. Tulio suspected his family would pick up Carlitos at any moment. He had to convince him to return to school the next day before he left. Suddenly, Tulio looked straight ahead, stood perfectly still, lifted a finger in the air, and let out a loud fart. Carlitos finally laughed.

"Let's go home," Tulio said, "Tomorrow when we come back to school, and you need to take a piss, raise your hand like this," Tulio showed him how, raising Carlitos' arm, "And, say, 'bathroom, please.' You've got to come back to school. We need to get to the eighth grade. I think we can then go to the movie school to be real movie stars." Carlitos placed a hand on Tulio's shoulder as they walked, perhaps in gratitude or maybe a child's loving gesture. Before the moment lingered, Tulio stopped walking and lifted his finger in the air again. Carlitos knew what came next and jumped out of Tulio's way laughing.

Chapter 7: Sleeping Alone

Young Carlos, now fourteen, stood in front of the bathroom mirror, dabbing on makeup for his school play role. His boyish good looks were perfect for the part. He inherited Facundo's height and wavy hair. He had Blanca's face along with her dreamy eyes. He had a splendid physique and a secure stride like his Papa.

Facundo walked past the open door, stopped, and asked, "What do you think you are doing?"

"It's for the school play, Papa. I'm going to be Peter Pan."

"Peter Pan? Who the hell is Peter Pan?"

Carlos did not have time to answer, "He's—"

"Wipe that off your face before somebody sees you are wearing women's makeup," he ordered.

Blanca overheard the exchange and yelled from her bedroom, "It's a costume, Facundo. All the students do it. He's been planning this for weeks."

"For weeks? You've been planning this for weeks?" asked Facundo, "Why can't you be a firefighter or a police officer? What the hell's the matter with being a cowboy?"

A car horn sounded, and someone yelled out, "Carlos!" Blanca stepped between Facundo and Carlos and said, "There's your ride, Carlos. You can't keep them waiting. Grab your books and lunch and go!" Carlos ran out the front door, leaving Blanca and Facundo standing in the hallway.

"I don't like this. I don't like this at all. I'm taking Carlos out of that Loretto School. He's coming with me to the ranch," warned Facundo as Blanca slammed her bedroom door behind her.

Facundo stood in silence in the hallway, then made his way toward Blanca's bedroom door. He slowly turned the doorknob and suddenly burst the door open, surprising Blanca, who stood naked, about to step in the shower. She reached for the doorknob, but Facundo got there first and flung the door wide open with a loud bang. Blanca remained still, not knowing what to expect. He came up from behind and placed his hands around her neck. Holding her captive, he whispered in her ear, "You haven't put out for a while? Don't you like screwing with me anymore?" He asked her aggressively.

"Don't be ridiculous, Facundo. A woman doesn't feel close to a man who treats her poorly. The thought of sex with you is disgusting. Treat a woman with respect, and she will give her life for you. That's what you should be teaching Carlos. Any cowboy can show him how to ride a stupid horse."

Facundo released the hold from around Blanca's neck. "Don't you know there's pussy everywhere? Women fuck me anytime I want. You want to play hard to get? Fine, you can sleep alone from now on."

Sidestepping Facundo, she wrapped a towel around herself, "Go with whatever whore you want."

Facundo's marriage to Blanca was like a tight noose around his neck. A nagging reminder of his hasty marriage to Blanca without proper legal counsel. A divorce now would entail sharing the accumulated affluence of three generations with her unless Blanca agreed to a waiver, and she was not negotiating. Facundo's father pleaded on his deathbed for him not to squander the family's wealth on something shameful as a divorce. Blanca was fearless and independent, and there was little Facundo could do about it. Blanca knew it and seemed to enrage him purposefully. He would retaliate by hurting all the things she loved. That included breaking young Carlos.

Chapter 8: Jesse and The Picnic in the Park

Everyone always knew when Sister Anne was approaching as her rosary beads jingled with each step of her foot. As she stood in the front of Carlos's classroom with her hands tucked under her nun's bib, she addressed Carlos's class. "Students, the annual picnic and graduation dance is next Friday. And students, it's a Friday. What does that mean for us Catholics?" asked the nun.

"No meat on Fridays!" replied the class in unison.

"That's right! No meat in your picnic lunches, but you can bring fish," the Sister said.

Jesse, a good-looking, hunky student, always sat in the back of the classroom. Today he wore a white tee-shirt, tight jeans, and his imitation leather jacket. He raised his hand and yelled out, "All we have at home is baloney. So, that means I won't be coming to school that day."

Sister Anne replied, "Jesse, of course, you will come. Let's talk about this after class. We will figure something out."

Carlos raised his hand and said, "I can bring an extra sandwich if Jesse likes tuna." Tulio slapped Carlos's back of the head, whispering low, "*Ay, Hussy.*"

Sister Anne added, "Isn't that a beautiful gesture? That's what the Lord wants. Good Christians to share their gifts with others while expecting nothing in return."

Tulio, giggling, could barely get out, "Expecting nothing in return. You hear that, sandwich queen?"

Sister Anne added, "Now, you say thank you to Carlos, Jesse."

Jesse stared at Carlos with a look of surprise and but said nothing.

"Immediately following the picnic, we will hold our graduation dance in the cafeteria. So, bring your favorite records. And remember, no cheek-to-cheek dancing. You must dance twelve inches apart. I will have my measuring tape with me," said the Sister over a chorus of boos.

Carlos and Tulio's friendship was uncommonly mature for their age. They supported each other's happiness with an implicit acceptance of each other's preferences – in food, games, movies, and music. Whatever one liked was okay with the other.

Their sexual awareness developed with no insight whatsoever into gay behavior or lifestyles. They had never seen a gay man. They heard stories about el Tino, who was the town's butt of jokes and ridicule. Forever misunderstood, he wandered Agua Prieta wearing heavy makeup. Nobody would give him a job. To support himself, he tried reading tarot cards and odd jobs. When that didn't work out, he started selling sexual favors to late-night, inebriated passersby. One morning, the garbage collector found his body in an empty lot with a metal wire around his neck. Some said it was murder, and others said he died of suicide. The authorities never cared to investigate the cause of his death.

When young girls flirted with Carlos and Tulio, they admitted to each other that they did not feel like kissing them like all the other boys said they did. Carlos and Tulio first started talking about their admiration for the student quarterback and basketball star. Their conversations slowly evolved into praise for their physical attributes—their eyes, face, legs, and torso. Then they started sharing fantasies of make-believe boyfriends and love for men with a yearning to have the love returned in kind.

One day, Tulio shared with Carlos his desire to openly go steady with a boy and sit on the schoolyard bench holding hands like all the other couples. "I would wear his class ring for everyone to see," said Tulio.

Carlos replied, "I would like a kiss from a boy like Troy Donahue kissed Sandra Dee in 'A Summer Place.'" Just like they first discovered their love for the theater in the basement of Tulio's home, now they also shared a mutual passion for men.

Fantasies about kissing boys were at odds with their religion and family values. Their chats needed to remain secret. So wrong, and yet it felt so right. It was not like any teenage crush. It felt so real – like something within them you can't control—and If you could, how would you go about it? The two young boys were on their own. They would have to make it up as they went along. At least they had each other.

Chapter 9: The Secret Hideaway

The Fifteenth Street Park in Douglas, Arizona, was only a block away from Loretto School. The students walked to the park supervised by Sister Anne. They broke up into groups and began playing games. Carlos and Tulio were on opposing volleyball teams. Carlos stuck out his tongue at Tulio through the volleyball net, who bent over and pointed to his butt, "Eat this, Carlos!"

"No thanks, *pedorro*. Shut up and play ball," said Carlos

Around noontime, Sister Anne rang a handbell announcing lunchtime, "It's lunchtime, students. Pick up your lunch boxes and stand quietly to say grace." The students stood at attention with their lunch and waited. "All together, now. Bless us, O Lord, and these thy gifts which we are about to receive from thy bounty through Christ, our Lord. Amen."

"You may have lunch, but you cannot leave the park nor cross the street," added the Sister, "I want all of you fully visible. I need to see where you are at all times. Don't make me come and find you."

Jesse leaned against a tree trunk, listening to Sister Anne and monitoring Carlos as he picked up their lunch. Carlos saw Jesse looking at him and walked over to where he stood. He opened the lunch bag and offered Jesse a wrapped homemade sandwich. Jesse took the sandwich with a hint of embarrassment and kept his eyes fixed on Carlos, "Let's get out of here." said Jesse.

"What? No! Sister Anne will kill us."

"You scared?"

"No, it's just that I don't want to." He hesitated, "Well, where do you want to go?"

"Just shut up and follow me," Jesse said, walking away.

Carlos followed Jesse and looked back to make sure Sister Anne wasn't watching. Jesse walked into a bush's narrow opening, protecting his face with his hands, and emerged on the other side. He waited for a moment and said, "What are you waiting for? Just cover your face with your hands and walk through the bush. Come on, Carlos!"

Carlos stepped into the bush and struggled to come out on the other side. Jesse pulled on his arm until he cleared the branches and was standing next to him, surrounded by a forest of thick shrubbery.

"Wow. This is like a secret hideaway. How did you find this place?" asked Carlos.

Jesse sat on the grass and unwrapped his sandwich, "I know many secret places."

"You come here a lot?" asked Carlos, sitting down next to Jesse.

"Yeah. It's a good place to bring chicks and talk them into letting me screw them."

"Do they, Jesse? Do they let you?"

"Always," Jesse answered. "But I have my ways."

"Ways?"

"Yeah, ways. Want to know how?"

"Okay, tell me."

"First, you pick a girl that's pretty. Then, you're really nice to her for a few days. I mean, really, really nice. Once you figure she thinks you have a crush on her, you ask if she wants to see a secret place."

"I bet most of them say yes to you," Carlos added.

"Well, wait. When you get here, you tell her she is really pretty and hold her hand. Then you kiss her hand. Next, you kiss her on the cheek, and finally, you kiss her on the lips as you slip your hand under the dress."

Carlos handed Jesse a soda bottle and an opener. Jesse popped open the soda and took a long swig before taking a large bite from his sandwich. He continued talking with his mouth full.

"Now, this is the tricky part. When you work your hand up her dress, you really want to pull down her panties. Although Ivonne Lopez? Do you know who I mean? Yeah, she doesn't wear any panties. So, it was a snap for me to get in there. She has a really hairy pussy."

"Come on, and they just let you take off their panties?"

"Well, wait, so she doesn't say stop, stop, stop, you kiss her nonstop. Don't even let her speak or say a word. Just kiss and pull and kiss and pull down their panties."

"I've never even kissed a girl – ever," admitted Carlos.

"I'm a great kisser. Yeah. All the girls love kissing me." Jesse boasted.

Carlos stared at Jesse's lips as he took the last bite of his tuna sandwich. He then took a long swig of his soda and placed his hand on Carlos's shoulder as he rubbed his crotch like relieving an itch.

"I could show you how. How to be a real good kisser."

"How?"

"Well, we could practice."

"On each other? Isn't that a sin?"

"Bullshit. It's fun. Besides, it's not like you're going to get knocked up," said Jesse.

"I don't know, and Sister Anne would..."

"So, what's going to happen when you're on a date and have to kiss a girl? You won't know how. Ha-ha!" sneered Jesse.

"I guess I..."

"It has to be done with your eyes closed."

"Oh, come on! Really?"

"Yes, you've got to close your eyes. Come on, close your eyes." Carlos closed his eyes.

"Now, when you feel my lips on yours, don't try to kiss me back. I hate that. Just hold still at first, then suck on my lower lip and tongue when I tell you. Ready?"

"Ready."

Jesse moved closer and held Carlos's face with both his hands. First, he brushed his lips across Carlos's and then kissed him with soft pecks on his lips. He then engulfed his lips with an open mouth and kissed him. Jesse smelled like Old Spice aftershave and tasted like the first sip of a bubbly Cola to Carlos, who sat motionless as Jesse prolonged the kiss, and then he embraced Jesse's lips with his.

Out of nowhere, they heard Tulio's voice, "Carlos! Where are you? Everyone is looking for you."

Carlos jumped up in a panic and ran back through the bushes without saying a word to Jesse. Tulio spotted Carlos emerging from the greenery and ran over to him. "Where the hell were you? I've been telling Sister Anne you were in the bathroom for over an hour."

"I was having lunch with Jesse."

"Behind the bushes?"

"Yeah."

"Oh my god, this is going to be good."

"You won't believe it," said Carlos.

"Oh, yes, I will. I'm all ears."

Chapter 10: The Bike Ride

After the picnic in the park, the students danced to music from a portable record player. Boys danced with girls, and some girls danced with girls. Nuns supervised the dance while measuring with a ruler for twelve inches of separation between dancers. Carlos and Tulio were excellent dancers. Girls would come up and ask them to dance. But today, after the park incident, they stood talking and listening to the music as they watched the dancers.

"I don't see Jesse. You think he's coming?" asked Tulio.

"I don't know. Maybe he doesn't like dancing," replied Carlos

"What if he shows up and asks you to dance?"

"Shut up."

"Well, would you dance with him?"

"Of course not. I'm not crazy."

"I would. Girls dance with girls, and boys can't?"

The students screamed as they formed a line with the first notes of "The Stroll." Carlos and Tulio joined the dance lineup and began moving to the music. As the song got underway, the loud sound of a motorcycle came from the outside. Sister Anne walked to the window and looked out, "Why, if it isn't Jesse on a motorcycle?"

Jesse was circling the perimeter of the school's playground on his motorcycle, stopping in front of the cafeteria entrance, revving up the bike, and yelling, "Carlos, come out! Carlos." Carlos, Tulio, and the students rushed to the windows to watch Jesse on his bike.

"Get out there. He's calling you. This is so cool," said Tulio

"Cool? This is embarrassing. Who does he think he is? Now everyone will start asking about the park," replied Carlos.

"Walk out like nothing ever happened. Be cool, man, otherwise everyone will really want to know what's going on."

"But I don't even know what going on," said Young Carlos.

"Get out there or else."

Carlos walked across the cafeteria with a determination like he'd seen in Facundo's outbursts and stopped directly in front of Jesse and his bike, "What are you doing? Are you crazy?" He asked. "Stop it!"

Jesse looked at Carlos defiantly and revved the bike again.

"Stop," pleaded Carlos, "Please, this is embarrassing."

"Get on," demanded Jesse and revved the bike again.

"What?"

"Get on!"

"No, I've never ridden a bike before."

"Get on."

"I don't know how to ride. Damn it, Jesse!"

Carlos looked over his shoulder and saw his classmates' faces at the windows and Sister Anne heading their way. He mounted the bike behind Jesse, holding his hands in the air, "How do I stay on? What do I hold on to?" asked Carlos in a panic.

"Me," said Jesse

With a quick jolt, the bike started moving. Carlos wrapped his arms around Jesse and held on tight, shielding his face from the wind against his shoulder. As they gained speed, a newfound sense of security came over him, holding onto Jesse. Excitement ran through his body like an electric current. They rode away in silence as the late afternoon sun cast long shadows all around them.

They cruised down G Avenue past the Douglas Drug, where young people hung out after school, then back to Fifteenth Street past St. Luke's Church towards the park. Jesse pulled into the park and carefully camouflaged the bike behind thick shrubs, setting the mood for a private encounter. They said nothing, took each other's hand, and together crossed the bushes into the interior of the secret hideout.

Jesse sat on the ground and gestured for Carlos to sit next to him. He then guided him to rest his head on his shoulder, letting out a deep sigh as he finally held Carlos in his arms. He kissed his face, eyes, and hair over and over, initiating his proven seduction technique.

Carlos looked up at the sky and pointed to the silhouette of the moon. "Look, Jesse, the moon is out in the daytime. It's good luck when you spot it! Did you know the moon and stars are always there, but we can't see them because the sun is so bright it drowns them out?"

"No, I didn't know that," Jesse said, squinting as he looked up at the sky.

"And the moon is never really yellow. It's just stuff flying around in the air that makes it look like it changes color."

"Really? I didn't know that for sure," replied Jesse, who would never entertain talk about anything like this. Who gives a shit why the moon changes colors? But today felt just right to wonder about the moon and stars. Why did Carlos hold his attention? He could watch him doing the simplest everyday tasks and constantly fought the urge to stare at him all the time. Now, here he was, right in his arms – all his.

Carlos seemed so unaware of himself. There was a sweet naivety that paused Jesse from acting out the more basic instincts he had in mind when he brought him here today. Something wasn't going according to plan. Something Jesse couldn't explain but could quickly spoil and would never want to. Now, if time could just stand still as they sat together, talking about the moon and prolonging the magic, captives of each other's presence.

"I need to get home before dark," said Carlos, lifting his head from Jesse's shoulder. They kissed as Jesse's hand worked its way to unbutton Carlos's pants and his. Jesse took off his shirt, placed it on the grass, and pulled his pants and shorts to his knees. Carlos sat with his pants unbuttoned. He was unsure of what to do. Jesse stood in front of him, straddling his legs with his hard cock inches away from his face, "Touch it." He said.

Carlos put his hand around Jesse's cock and stroked it awkwardly. He had never seen a cut penis before and wasn't sure if he could hurt it. Jesse kneeled in front of him, pulled Carlos's pants off, and pushed him onto his back on the grass. He lay on top of him while kissing his neck and lips. "Have you ever been butt fucked?" whispered Jesse kissing his ear. Carlos shook his head. "Can I do that to you?" he asked as he lifted Carlos's legs over his shoulders. "It hurts a little at first, but if you relax once I'm in, then it's a lot of fun."

Jesse came prepared with a small bottle of Jergen's almond-scented lotion. He rubbed the fragrant lotion on his dick and Carlos's butt hole before he slowly began entering him. Carlos groaned but did not pull away. He was intoxicated by the lotion's scent and Jesse's panting. "Relax, relax," Jesse repeated in a voice trembling with excitement until he climaxed with a heavy sigh. He kept his dick inside, rubbing Carlos's cock until he came. He kissed Carlos and sighed with pleasure as he pulled out. Then reached for a roll of toilet paper he kept on the motorcycle, cleaned himself, and offered it to Carlos.

"Now you have something of me inside you," Jesse said with a smirk. Carlos knew what Jesse wanted, but it all happened so fast. He wasn't sure he liked playing a woman's role during sex with Jesse. Carlos liked boys but was vigilant of never looking effeminate.

"You owe me one," Carlos responded as he cleaned up and zipped his pants.

It was early evening when they pulled up to Carlos's home. Carlos got off the bike and stood next to Jesse. Neither spoke for a few seconds.

"I can pick you up for school tomorrow morning," said Jesse with a soft voice Carlos had never heard him use before and didn't respond. "Come on, man," Jesse added, "I'll bring you back after school too."

"You scare me, Jesse. This whole thing scares me."

"Don't you like me?"

"Yes, I like you a lot. That scares me even more."

"Good, because I want to do this again and again. Can't you keep a secret?"

"Yes, my father would kill me if I didn't. I'm serious."

Jesse ignored the comment and started up the bike, "Nothing will happen to you as long as I'm around. Be outside tomorrow morning by eight."

Young Carlos followed him with his eyes as he pulled away, confused about all that just happened. It happened so fast. He turned and walked up to his front door in a daze. As he turned the doorknob, he heard Facundo's voice in the background. A wave of fear washed over him. The dreamlike moment was over, and now reality lay ahead.

Dear Young Carlos,

37

You are in love! The most important question to ask your lover is if I tell you the worst about me, would you still love me? Would you still like the person I am when nobody's watching? A truthful answer requires you always to be yourself. Don't pretend through anything. True love flourishes when you are so completely yourself that everyone feels that they can be themselves.

Jesse isn't perfect. There is deep bonding in accepting a lover's shortfalls. Create a safe space to talk about anything, just like you and Tulio.

Jesse thinks of himself as a superhero. He needs you to see him in that light. When he satisfies you sexually, he feels like a winner. Let him know that you like it. Sex should feel good for him and you. There is embarrassment, funny noises, odd smells, but it should be fun. Always ask for consent before initiating any sexual activity and remember, you can say "no" or "slow down" whenever it becomes too much for you.

Your newfound sexual desires are an opportunity to build the discipline of self-control. Exercising discretion preserves intimate moments' pleasure – otherwise, you debase the beauty of intimacy. Never initiate anything you won't look back on with honor. You have a gut that acts as an inner voice. Listen to it.

It's fantastic to be in love.

Your Elder Self.

Chapter 11: Paloma and The Affair

Paloma didn't put up with any live-in boyfriend once they stopped spending money on her. She would pile their possession onto the curb, change her locks on the very morning after they didn't come home, and start looking for better prospects. When Paloma crossed paths with Facundo, a wealthy married man sitting alone at the bar, it was like finding the goose that lays the golden eggs. She befriended him, and he seized the opportunity. They were becoming fast friends by providing each other something of value. He would spend money, and she took him back to her place as a reward.

Paloma was an expert at keeping a man on the hook. Facundo liked role-playing, something Blanca would never consider. She was game for everything. He couldn't wait to get to her place for her to dress up as a schoolgirl and pretend he was teaching her all about sex for the very first time or see her lean over in the nun's costume wearing nothing underneath. She would tie him up and slather him with whipping cream and lick it all off. At the end of each encounter, Facundo would return home to his family, a habit Paloma was determined to break.

Facundo and Paloma sat at the Santa Fe Bar drinking mezcal shots and listening to mariachis play *"Paloma Negra."* Facundo, with an arm around Paloma, appeared intoxicated. She took a long gulp of her mezcal and yelled out, *"Ay, Ay, Ay."*

"That's what I like, a happy woman," slurred Facundo.

"Happy? Yes. But I'm not going to be your girlfriend forever," she said as she waved her hand in Facundo's face. She spread her fingers and asked, "What's missing here? A ring or no more pussy for you." She said. Facundo hugged her close and kissed her.

Just then, Tulio walked into the bar and headed to the carryout window. He stood waiting for his order, checking out the bar scene, and saw Facundo kissing Paloma. He quickly looked the other way, but Paloma caught him staring at them, "Look, Facundo. There's your son's little sissy friend looking at us. I hope he tells your wife."

Tulio grabbed his takeout order and rushed out. With one long shot of mezcal and a kiss to Paloma, Facundo got up and started walking unsteadily to the door. As Facundo walked away, Paloma yelled sarcastically. "You are so henpecked that you cackle when you walk."

When Facundo walked outside, he looked around, but Tulio was long gone. Facundo got in his truck and checked for bullets in the forty-five he always carried in his glove compartment. Then he drove off in the direction of his home.

Facundo avoided parking in the driveway. Instead, he parked on the curb outside the home for an easier get-away. Taking the handgun from the glove compartment, he made his way to the front door and walked in as quietly as he could, checking rooms for any sign of Carlos or Bonita. He overheard the sound of a sewing machine coming from Blanca's bedroom. Blanca thought she heard the front door.

"Carlos, is that you? Bonita?"

Facundo wobbled into Blanca's bedroom and stood at the doorway, hiding the gun behind his back.

"Sorry to disappoint you. It's just me."

"You're drunk again? Get out of my room," she said, getting up from her sewing chair.

"Why so unfriendly? I just came by for a little visit. Just you and me this time."

Meanwhile, Jesse and Carlos rounded the corner on the motorcycle approaching Carlos's home. Carlos saw his father's truck parked in front and immediately felt dread.

"I've gotta go. My father is probably drunk. He gets crazy when he's drunk."

"You want me to come with you? I'll beat the living shit out of him," said Jesse.

"No, no," answered Carlos. He jumped off the bike and ran past the front door and into Blanca's bedroom, where Blanca cowered in a corner as Facundo was kicking and hitting her.

"Stop! Leave her alone!" yelled Carlos, shielding Blanca from Facundo. He stooped down to help her up and saw her bloody nose and a bruised forehead. Facundo's breath and exertion filled the bedroom with a smell of violence and stale liquor.

"Why don't you pick on someone your size?" yelled Young Carlos.

"You're about my size. Want to have a go at it?" Facundo said, "Or are you a Mama's boy?" Facundo imitated a baby crying, "WHAA WHAA. Where's my mama?"

"Go back to the ranch. You know you don't belong here anymore," yelled Carlos.

"Oh, yeah? I don't belong here. You want to starve to death?" He replied jeeringly.

Carlos saw the revolver Facundo was hiding with one hand behind his back, "Are you going to use that on me? Go ahead, and they'll put you away for life. All your money and you will rot in jail for the rest of your life."

"You ungrateful piece of shit," replied Facundo.

Picking up his mother from the floor, he said, "You won't fix things with a few pesos this time around."

Facundo stood with his fists clenched and was ready to throw a punch. Carlos remained firm, looking at his father straight in the eyes. They stood in front of each other like two pitted roosters before a cockfight. After a few tense moments, Facundo turned to leave, bumping into the wall and door on the way out. He cursed the door and everyone in the house it belonged to and stormed out. Carlos remained still listening for Facundo's footsteps, and when he heard the truck engine start, he turned to help Blanca onto her bed.

"You saved my life, Carlos. You did. He is so drunk. One more minute, and he was going to kill me." Blanca said in a trembling voice.

"Shh. Shh. Let me get the first aid kit."

"He really was, and you know what was going through my mind? That you or Bonita would be the ones to find my body. That would be the last memory of your mother," she added with a sob.

Carlos brought a first aid kit and began dabbing the wounds with cotton and sanitizer, "Be still. Let me clean these cuts up. This might hurt."

"Nothing hurts anymore," replied Blanca.

Bonita arrived and, as she walked into the room, said, "Oh, god. What happened here?"

"Papa. You know," answered Carlos.

Bonita, clearly angered, looked around and said, "Where is he?"

"Gone." Blanca replied, "I'm okay. I'm okay."

"We need to take her to the hospital," said Bonita.

"No! No hospital," said Blanca.

"Why do you put up with this, Mama?" Bonita asked again.

"I know it's bad. I've got to figure something out," replied Blanca.

"You leave him, Mama. That's what you do," pleaded Bonita, "You've got to do it. I will never let a man treat me like that."

Blanca patted the bed with her hand, signaling for Bonita and Carlos to sit at her side. "If I leave your father, he will pick up the first skirt he sees walking down the street, take up with her and give her children. And those kids will have the life that rightfully belongs to you two. He will never look back. Loyalty is not a part of his world. I've got to hang on a little longer. You will go to excellent schools and become somebody."

"We'll be okay. I'll get a job," said Carlos

"I can work at the drugstore," said Bonita.

"Why do I have to go away to school? I like it here better," added Carlos.

"Mama, I don't even like school. I want to marry Luis and have a big wedding. That's all I want. I wouldn't be any good at an expensive school," added Bonita.

The pink princess phone by Blanca's bed started ringing. Carlos picked it up and muttered, "Hello?"

"And what is the lady of the house doing?" joked Tulio on the other end.

"Not now, Tulio. It's not a good time."

"Is everything alright?"

"Yeah, I'm just busy. Why do you ask?"

"It's probably nothing. I'll tell you tomorrow at school."

"Jesse stuff?" Carlos whispered.

"No, no, it's not about your hunk."

"Tomorrow is the last day of school. So, you have all summer to tell me."

"I see you doing a lot of biking this summer," then added, "You should get a bike yourself. You and Jesse could ride together. How butch. Anyway, we'll chat later."

Carlos hung up the phone and paused for a minute in deep thought, then asked, "Mama, do you think I could get a motorcycle?"

Dear Young Carlos,

Facundo and Blanca, at one time, were young and naïve -- just like you. They had dreams and passionate desires. They also had difficult times with their parents when they didn't get along. There is a child within them that is still trying to be happy and wanting to be loved,

If you remember your parents as children with unfulfilled dreams, you will better understand why they act the way they do. When you see them disagree, they defend their dream, just like when you stand up for being a movie star. They do not mean to hurt you.

Your Papa and Mama will chart their own life's course. You cannot alter their path. You can, however, be an understanding heart that hopes their dreams come true. Love them. That's the best you can do.

Your Elder Self.

Chapter 12: The Graduation

Sister Anne stood at a podium in front of a student assembly, testing the microphone. She softly tapped the mouthpiece to check the volume level. The tapping traveled through the speakers and served as a call to attention for the students. Carlos and Tulio sat with the graduating eighth-grade class. Jesse sat three rows back, a choice that made Carlos wonder if he didn't like to be out with him and Tulio in public.

Sister Anne welcomed the students, "My dear students, the Sisters and I are very proud of your achievements this year as always. Some of you excelled in academics and personal development. As is our tradition, we will now give the awards for academic achievement, perfect attendance, and the big award for the spirit of Catholicism. Please come up when I call your name to receive your award." The students applauded and cheered.

Carlos whispered to Tulio, "What was it you wanted to tell me?" Tulio hesitated a few seconds, "I don't remember. It was nothing. I'm sorry I opened my big mouth."

"Now I'm really curious, and you have to tell me."

Tulio checked around for anyone listening and said, "Okay, have you heard of a woman named Paloma?"

"Is this another woman you suspect is really a man?"

"No, no." Tulio hesitated and moved closer to whisper in Carlos's ear, "She drinks and then sleeps around."

Just then, Sister Anne announced the winner of the spirit of Catholicism award. The students applauded, and a young lady walked to the front of the hall where Sister Anne was standing with the special award. As the applause started to die down, Carlos turned to Tulio, "So? What about this Paloma?"

"They say she's your Papa's girlfriend."

"Bullshit," replied Carlos.

"I saw them kissing at the Santa Fe Bar."

Carlos looked straight ahead and remained silent, pretending his attention was on the ceremony.

"I am sorry I said anything. Okay?" said Tulio.

"Every father in town plays around, Tulio. Name me one who doesn't."

Sister Anne was finishing up the ceremonies, "That concludes our year-end ceremonies. Congratulations to all, and may your summer be joyful and filled with the blessings of the Lord. Rise for our last prayer" The students stood and began in unison: "Our father who art in heaven, hallowed be thy name. Thy kingdom comes, they will be done..."

After the prayer, the room erupted with cheers. Students hugged and said their goodbyes to one another. As they walked outside, Jesse waited for Carlos at a distance by his bike. "Target spotted. Directly behind you," whispered Tulio when he spotted Jesse.

Carlos walked over to Jesse, "Guess what? I think I might get a bike."

"Oh, yeah? You could've had this one."

"No, dummy. Another bike to ride together."

"That'll never happen."

"Why? Are you ashamed of being seen with me?"

"How can you ask me that? I made a fool of myself just to get you on my bike. Remember?" he replied. "Truth is, my old lady can't find work here. It's been tough, so we are moving to L.A."

"What? You're moving to L.A. When?"

"In a couple of days. We're taking the Amtrak. I've never been on a train."

"You are moving that fast? How long have you known?"

Jesse hesitated, darting his eyes, then looked down and fiddled with his keys. "A while now. Ma was just waiting for me to finish the school year."

"You could have said something sooner, Jesse," Carlos said.

"Then you wouldn't have liked me, and I liked you already."

"Of course, I would like you. I would like you, anyway. How many times do you have to hear me say it?"

"Zillions," said Jesse.

Carlos chuckled and asked, "Do you remember how I taught you to say I love you in Spanish?"

"Te quiero," replied Jesse with a thick accent, "I sold the bike and have to drop it off later. Do you want to go for one last ride?"

Carlos ran to where Tulio was standing and handed him his schoolbooks, "Bad news. Can you keep these for me? I'll call you later tonight."

"What? Tell me, tell me," replied Tulio.

"No time. I will stop by later."

He got behind Jesse on the bike, and they rode away toward their hideaway.

Chapter 13: The Car Chase

Facundo and Paloma kissed as they said goodbye at the Brookhill Bar. As Paloma got in her car, she saw Blanca's car drive by. Suspecting Blanca might be stalking them, she decided to follow her. As Blanca stopped at a red light, Paloma sped up and bumped her rear fender. Blanca's head jerked forward and then stuck her head out, "Hey! Watch your driving."

Paloma yelled back, "I just screwed your husband five minutes ago."

Blanca stepped on the gas pedal to leave Paloma's car behind, but Paloma was tipsy. She accelerated and stayed close behind her, bumping her rear fender and yelling obscenities. Blanca raced home and turned into her driveway. As Paloma passed the house, she yelled, "I'm going to give your husband the crabs. So, keep your legs crossed. Ha-ha!"

Blanca sat in the car and took a few deep breaths. As she walked into the house, Bonita and Carlos were watching American Bandstand. Blanca put down her shopping bags and sighed.

"What's the matter, Mama?" Bonita asked, "You look flustered."

"This awful woman in a blue car followed me home yelling obscenities about your father and bumping my rear fender with her car," she answered and made her way down the hallway towards her bedroom.

"I know who that is," said Carlos.

"Who?" Bonita asked.

"Her name is Paloma. She meets up with Papa at the Santa Fe Bar. Tulio saw them kissing."

"Wait. So, all this time, we think Papa is at the ranch, he's here in town?"

"I guess."

Carlos followed Bonita into her mother's bedroom, "Why do you put up with this, Mama? Why do you allow it? We can make it without him," said Bonita.

Blanca put away items from a shopping bag and sat on the bed. "Women like me have no options. Marriage is the only solution. Your papa is like someone with whom I've grown older, gotten to know, and now is someone else. It's hard to explain how that works, how you can wind up bonded to someone you've known so well who now someone is else," she said.

"Papa's abusive here but goes out and has a good time with another woman?" asked Carlos.

"Your papa is an angry man, that much we know. He was never a child, he never played, and started working when he was twelve years old." She paused, looking for signs of empathy on her children's faces, and then continued. "I knew his parents had to pressure him into marrying me, but I went along because he was my only chance at a new life. I later found out he had a girlfriend he loved. His behavior is unacceptable, but as a woman, I somehow understand it. His anger is a cry for freedom."

"Yeah, it's not Papa's fault. It's this woman who baits him for money. That makes me so angry. How can someone try to break up a home?" said Bonita.

Blanca smiled and said, "You won't understand now, but one day you will. Stop worrying about it. This is not your fault. It's ours. Only ours."

Later that evening, Bonita and Carlos quietly pushed Blanca's car from the driveway onto a safe distance from the house. They jumped in, and Bonita started the vehicle.

"Go slow, go slow! Someone will see us," said Carlos.

"You are sure they meet at the Santa Fe Club?"

"No, I'm not sure. That's where Tulio saw them together."

Bonita and Carlos arrived at the Santa Fe Club and parked near the front door. There was no sign of Facundo's truck nor a blue car parked anywhere. They waited in silence, hunched in the front seat of Blanca's car, hoping to remain unseen. Soon, the blue car with Paloma arrived and parked a few cars down from Blanca's car.

"There she is," said Bonita, "Quick. Take off your belt."

"What? Why?"

"Just give me your damn belt!"

Carlos took off his leather belt and handed it to Bonita.

"You won't like this, so just stay here in the car," warned Bonita and jumped out as Paloma locked her car door. She saw Bonita approaching but had no idea she was hiding a leather belt behind her back.

"Well, if it isn't my boyfriend's daughter," she said, "Are you here for some pesos from Papa?"

Bonita came closer to Paloma and, without a word, suddenly slashed her across the back with the belt. Paloma screamed and arched her back. Bonita whipped her again, and Paloma cried out as she tried to turn the locked car door.

"You like to mess with my family, do you? Let's settle this between us girls. Come close to my mama again, and I will find you wherever you are, *cabrona.*" She said, giving her one more strike as Paloma finally got in her car and locked the door. She pulled out in her car without even checking for oncoming traffic and sped away. Bonita stood in the parking spot, panting, the belt hanging from her hand. Carlos came up to her, took the belt, and began putting it back on, "You are brave, sister," he said.

"Nah, it's just what needed to be done – a move right out of Papa's playbook. He always says you reward abuse with more abuse. I don't think Mama needs to worry about Paloma again. Let's go home."

Chapter 14: The Bumblebees

Two passenger trains came through Douglas, Arizona. The eight-fifteen morning train headed east towards Chicago and the five o'clock evening train to Los Angeles. Jesse's mother checked her train tickets for the number of their assigned car as she and Jesse made their way out to the waiting train towing their suitcases.

Carlos and Tulio ran past the Southern Pacific depot gates in a frantic search for Jesse, who walked alongside the train about to board with his mother at the far end of the platform. Jesse saw Carlos and started walking faster, "Jesse! Jesse! Wait up," yelled Carlos.

Tulio whistled so loud it even surprised Carlos, "Jesse!" shouted Tulio.

Jesse couldn't bear a big goodbye nor wanted any drama in front of his mother since he had never mentioned Carlos. He purposely hadn't said goodbye, knowing it would hurt Carlos and make it easier for him to forget the affair. Jesse would now act tough with him here at the station and be distant and pretend he had never cared. In time, Carlos would forget the hurt, the reason he cried, and the one who hurt him.

As Carlos and Tulio got closer, Jesse's mother heard his name called and said something to him as she boarded the train and disappeared inside. Jesse stepped onto the train and stood at the open car door, waiting for Carlos and Tulio to get to where he stood.

"I wasn't sure if you were leaving today, Jesse," said Carlos. Jesse continued his silence. "I'm going to miss you. *Adios,*" added Carlos with a lump in his throat.

"All Aboard! Tucson, Yuma, San Diego, and Los Angeles. All aboard, please!" Announced the conductor. "Sir," he said to Jesse as he walked by,

"Get inside your car and take your seat, please." Jesse remained standing at the doorway.

The final train whistle's haunting sound deepened their anxiety, and with a soft jolt, the train started moving. Jesse remained just inside the train doorway with eyes locked on Carlos. "Don't be sad. You'll find another boy. You've got money," said Jesse.

"I wish I had never gone to that picnic with you. Then, it wouldn't be so hard to say goodbye," said Carlos.

As the train picked up speed, Carlos started running to keep up, and Jesse's heart broke, and he could no longer hold his feelings in. He held his arm out to touch Carlos one last time. Carlos tried to reach his outstretched hand, but the train left him behind. Jesse yelled out to him, "You will always be that guy. *Te quiero. Te quiero.*" He remained in the open doorway, looking back at Carlos. The train whistled and gained full speed, turned, and Jesse disappeared.

Tulio caught up with Carlos, "You're going to be fine. You always are."

"Everyone always says that," replied Carlos wiping tears, "Like I didn't have feelings. Yes, I know I'm going to be okay. But right now, I'm sad and can't ever let anyone know why," said Carlos.

"Go ahead and cry. I'll cover for you," said Tulio looking around.

"I know why they say this is so wrong. Because it hurts so much, you don't think you can survive it."

"So be sad but remember that Jesse loves you. He tried to hide it, but he couldn't. I bet, right about now, he's in the train bathroom bawling his eyes out."

"That does not make me feel any better, Tulio."

"No?" asked Tulio

"No," repeated Carlos

Suddenly, Tulio stopped walking and stood still. He raised one finger in the air, let out a loud fart, and said, "Did you know the bumblebee is too fat to fly?"

"What?" replied Carlos

"Yeah, some guy discovered that the bumblebee's wings couldn't hold it up in the air. But since nobody told the bumblebee it couldn't fly, one day, it just took off."

"What are you talking about? Have you been drinking?" asked Carlos.

"We are like bumblebees. People think we won't find love, but they are so wrong. It will happen if we never once doubt it, just like the bumblebees. And you know what? Jesse's right. You will find someone else, and so will I. We're hot! We can double date. Summer's here, and I have a brand new hot pink swimsuit to show off at the Fifteenth Street pool."

Tulio walked around, flapping his arms and jumping up and down, "Look out world, here come the bumblebees!"

Carlos stared at Tulio in disbelief for a few moments and then said, "You know what, Tulio?"

"What?"

"I really love you. You are one of a kind."

"Okay, man, but right now, I think we should go to Dairy Queen – my treat. I heard they are having a twenty-nine-cent sale on banana splits, and nothing sounds more delicious than a big banana with whipped cream all over it. Yum!"

Dear Young Carlos,

Life is full of moments like this. Don't regret falling in love with Jesse. Don't regret a thing. Your moments together were so beautiful, you would do it all over again even if you knew this day would come.

Some you love will stay in your heart but not in your life. Some will leave you, and you still love them. Love is a powerful bond you can honor from far away. But also understand that love is not always enough to make a relationship last. Don't allow anything to stop you from being in love.

Never give up on Love,

Your Elder Self.

Chapter 15: Fend for Yourselves

Facundo threw clothes into two open suitcases. Carlos stood at the bedroom door, watching, "Are you going on a trip?" He asked, knowing that the answer could lead to confrontation. Facundo continued grabbing clothes and stuffed them in suitcases. "Where are you going?" Carlos insisted.

Facundo struggled to close the over-stuffed bags. Once he heard them click shut, he said, "I'm moving to the ranch. You can fend for yourselves."

"Fend for ourselves?"

"Until your mother agrees to my conditions, I am not paying for anything and closing all credit accounts, department stores, supermarkets, gas stations, and schools. You can figure out how to survive for yourselves."

"Mama isn't even here now. Why don't you wait to talk before you leave?"

"It won't be a surprise. However, you know better than to cross me. If you ever cross me again, know that I'll do something much worse to you." Carlos knew he meant the Paloma incident. Facundo took one last look around the room, picked up the suitcases, walked past Carlos, and out to his truck just as Blanca's car pulled into the driveway. He drove past her without even acknowledging her presence.

"Wow. Papa moved out and said he is not coming back," Carlos said to Blanca. "And that he was not supporting us anymore and closed all of our charge accounts."

Blanca replied, "I knew this day would come. I've been putting money away every week for years. We'll be fine for a while, but you and Bonita might need to get a part-time job."

Chapter 16: The Club Cupido

Carlos honked outside Tulio's home in his mother's car. If you knew the right people in Agua Prieta, you could get a driving permit at fourteen years of age. And tonight, he borrowed Blanca's car for the weekly meeting of Club Cupido. The club was a way for teenagers to meet and socialize in the small town. A brief business meeting preceded dancing and spending time with each other. Each year, the club selected a queen and held a summer coronation dance and a king for the Valentine's Day dance. Tonight, the members were voting on the Valentine Dance King.

Tulio ran out of his front door and got in the car with Carlos. He was wearing an eyeliner shade that accentuated his big green eyes and Chanel No.5 cologne. "I am nominating you for King," he said as soon as he sat down.

"No, don't!" said Carlos," It doesn't look good when your best friend nominates you."

"Okay, then I'll get Lucy to do it."

"I don't know, Tulio. I don't think I can survive getting excited and then disappointed if I don't win right now."

"Let me handle this. You'll see," said Tulio, pulling down the car's visor and checking himself out in the mirror, "Well, what do you think of my fresh look?"

"Fine by me. You've got beautiful eyes," said Carlos.

As the meeting got started, teenagers danced to records by "Los Apson Boys," a local band that made it big in Mexico. Luisa, the club president, asked for the music and dancing to stop.

"Okay, okay, everyone. Sit down. Today, we vote for the boy who will be the new king for Valentine's dance. So now, write down the name of a boy you would like to be king and put it in the hat."

Luisa held up a hat as teenagers began writing. Luisa collected the votes and called out names to Victoria, who acted as secretary and tallied them.

"Pepe, one vote."

"Tulio, one vote. "

"Carlos, one vote."

"Gustavo, one vote."

"Carlos, one vote."

"That's mine. That's my vote!" yelled Tulio

"Quiet, Tulio. It's supposed to be a secret!" said Victoria.

Luisa continued reading the paper ballots' names in the hat, "Pepe, Carlos, and the last vote goes to...Carlos! Madame Secretary, may I have the results?" asked Luisa. Victoria read off the totals.

"Gustavo, one vote. Memo, four votes. Pepe, ten votes. Tulio, one vote, and Carlos, thirteen votes. The new king is King Carlos!"

"Viva! King Carlos!" yelled Tulio, jumping up and down and holding Carlos's arm up in a victory gesture.

"Alright, everyone," said Luisa, "Now let's assign duties for the dance. It's only one month away."

Chapter 17: The Valentine's Dance

One month later, teenagers dressed in formal attire collected tickets at the Casino de Agua Prieta Hall door. The Club Cupido dances were well-attended events. Men in suits and women in dressy evening gowns of all ages came to dance until the early hours of the morning to music from a live orchestra. Blanca and Bonita sat at a table on the dancefloor's edge with an excellent view of the throne chair set up for Carlos's coronation.

Carlos stood with Tulio in a back room, waiting to hear his name called and make his way to the throne as the new Valentine's Day King. In a new short pixie haircut and light makeup, Tulio brought out a bottle of Chanel No.5 and sprayed it all over Carlos, who wore a red blazer, a white shirt, and black-tie. Carlos noticed that Tulio's makeup was a little heavier and his lip color a little darker. He said nothing.

"Stop. Enough cologne," said Carlos.

"It's never, ever enough," said Tulio, spraying the air all around them.

At the microphone, Luisa asked the orchestra to stop and dancers to take their seats.

"It is my honor to present the new king of Club Cupido Valentine's dance. Please welcome King Carlos."

Carlos walked out to applause and music. He circled the dance floor, giving shy waves before sitting on the throne chair. Luisa placed a crown on his head. Next, Carlos and Luisa took to the dancefloor and danced to the Blue Danube. The rest of the attendees joined half-way through the waltz. Dancers stopped Carlos to congratulate him with hugs and well wishes. The seven-piece orchestra changed up the rhythm to a fast cha-cha, and the party was on its way. Bonita danced to a couple of songs and then left with her boyfriend Luis to accompany Blanca home.

As the dance continued into the night, Carlos got up from his table to use the bathroom. Ever since his first-grade toilet accident at Loretto School, he wondered if he had a weak bladder. Dr. Valverde, sitting with his wife and two sons at a nearby table, watched Carlos walk by his table and go past the bathroom door. The doctor asked if anyone wanted anything from the bar and got up from his table. He walked past the bar and into the men's room.

Carlos was peeing into a urinal when he heard someone walk in. Dr. Valverde entered, checking for anybody else in the men's room. Seeing no one, he smiled and walked over to Carlos at the urinal.

"How does it feel to be a King?" asked the doctor sheepishly.

"It's fun, sir," Carlos answered absentmindedly, keeping his gaze on the urinal he was using.

Dr. Valverde moved uncomfortably close to Carlos at the urinal, "Is it true all kings have big dicks?" asked the doctor looking down at Carlos's penis and touching himself.

Carlos smiled with embarrassment and quickly zipped up. Suddenly, in a desperate move, the doctor spun him around to kiss him on the lips. Carlos pushed him away so forcefully that the doctor tumbled onto the bathroom floor, sending his glasses skidding across the room. Carlos rushed out the door as the doctor started getting back on his feet.

Once back at the table, he whispered the bathroom incident in Tulio's ear. Tulio's eyes opened wide. "Don't say a word, Tulio. There are no winners in this," said Carlos.

"Fucking, dirty, closet queen," said Tulio, looking toward Dr. Valverde's table.

"Shh, Tulio. Someone will hear you."

"Why should we cover for that old closet queen," Tulio said as the doctor passed by, adjusting his glasses. He stared at Carlos and Tulio with anger and sat at his table.

"Let's not ruin tonight. Besides, Papa says when someone says something about a person, even when it's a lie, it never goes away. So, let's not let this get out."

"He's right. Where there's smoke, there's fire," added Tulio, flashing dirty looks toward Dr. Valverde's table.

The well-known doctor could not afford the incident getting out. Fearful of repercussions, Dr. Valverde got ahead of the story by turning it around and accusing Carlos of making a pass at him in the men's bathroom. Mrs. Valverde appeared shocked and then laughed loud enough for Carlos and Tulio to hear. She turned to whisper the news to the table next to her. Carlos, unaware, danced happily, oblivious to the gossip spreading amongst the remaining late-night dancers.

As the evening wore on, Carlos needed the restroom again and alerted Tulio. "Okay, Tulio. I am going to risk the bathroom a second time."

"Want me to go with you?"

Carlos laughed, "No, I'm not a little girl."

"You should try carrying a bottle with a hose from your dick," laughed Tulio.

He got up and walked toward the bathroom. Dr. Valverde's two sons, Nacho and Poncho, nudged each other and got up from their table. As Carlos relieved himself, the two young men walked in. Nacho went directly up to where Carlos stood at the urinal. Turning him around, he punched his face and then his stomach while Poncho stood at the door, making sure nobody was coming. Carlos doubled forward in pain. When Nacho struck Young Carlos in the gut again, he fell to the floor.

"You faggot queer," said Nacho, spitting in his face as he opened his fly and began pissing on Carlos as he lay on the tiled floor. *"Puto!* This will teach you not to grab men in bathrooms," said Poncho. The two men quickly gave each other a quick thumbs up and ran out.

Tulio saw the two coming out of the bathroom laughing and got suspicious. He decided to check on Carlos and found him wiping urine and blood from his face with a bathroom paper towel. His white shirt was bloodied, he was drenched in urine, and his blazer was torn.

"What happened?" asked Tulio.

"I didn't expect that. They came out of nowhere," said Carlos. "They think I came onto Dr. Valverde." Tulio knew Carlos couldn't return to the dance floor in his condition. He had to get Carlos out of there unseen.

"Come on. Let's go home," said Tulio. "It's late anyway, and there are very few people left. I don't think anyone will find out," he said as he led Carlos out the Casino's back door, unaware that Dr. Valverde's version of the story was spreading to everyone like wildfire.

Chapter 18: People Never Forget

"**T**hey caught me by surprise," said Carlos as Blanca tended to his bruises.

"Don't worry," said Bonita, "I'll make sure the truth comes out about Dr. Valverde."

"Do nothing. It will only make matters worse," said Blanca.

"How can it get any worse, Mama?" asked Carlos

"It'll pass. People forget," replied Blanca.

"People will never forget about this," added Carlos

"You are safe here. You are always safe with us," said Bonita.

"I don't know, Mama. I suddenly feel like I no longer fit in. I don't fit in at home. I don't fit in at school. I don't fit in anywhere," said Carlos helplessly. He was going through a wide range of emotions, and they could see the underlying vulnerability.

"Yes, you do. People love you," said Bonita.

"Not anymore. People I've always known look at me like a stranger. I don't want to see anyone because I know how they feel inside about me."

"Nonsense. You are very popular," countered Blanca.

"No, Mama, listen to me. People who used to hide their dislike for me are now nasty and getting bolder. I'm not making this up. They make me feel ashamed, and I know I bring shame to you. What can I do? I can't disappear."

"Stop it!" yelled Bonita, "We will never be ashamed, no matter what! I am proud of you."

"No, listen. Will you and I be able to go to the store together? Will we? Without someone saying something mean for everyone to hear? How do you suppose that makes me feel?"

"I don't care what anyone says," said Bonita as she took Carlos's hand, "Brother, you know what you don't realize? They are jealous of you. I think you need some boxing lessons. That will make them go away."

"I guess I have to learn to act like I don't hurt inside. Maybe I should go away to school. But how can I risk leaving you with Papa around?"

"Let's give this a rest for now," said Blanca, "Let's think about what's best gently and pray for an answer and see what happens."

Blanca realized she needed to find a way for Carlos to start anew. A rustle in the trees outside caught her attention. She looked out to the elm tree she planted when they first arrived in town.

How the tree had grown. The branches of that tree had spread high and wide. She saw a mother bird nursing her trembling chick as it opened its beak, pleading for food. Blanca knew the mama bird would soon stop feeding and force the young bird to find its food or die as mandated by nature for each to survive.

"Thank you, Lord," whispered Blanca.

Chapter 19: The Fellow Drinker

Facundo sipped on a mug of beer at the Santa Fe Bar, listening to the bartender crack a gay joke, acting out in effeminate gestures.

"So, this *puto* had a crush on a young doctor and made an appointment saying he had a case of bad constipation. So, the *joto* stuck a dozen roses up his ass, and when the doctor pulled them out, he said, 'To you with all my love, doctor.'" Everyone at the bar roared with laughter.

"You sure know a lot of gay jokes," said one customer, "First-hand knowledge?" He added as the men laughed again.

"No, sir," replied the bartender, "I only get hard with women. Nothing could be worse than limp wrists." He said as he poured beer into a mug for a customer.

A fellow drinker came up and sat on the stool next to Facundo, "You and I, Facundo, are old friends, aren't we? We go back a long way."

"We sure do, *Compa*," replied Facundo, "We've done some good business and chased a few ladies here and there."

"It pains me to say this to you, but I just think, as a buddy, you need to know. I mean, damn, I would want to know."

"Of course, amigo. Tell me. Bartender, give us another round here."

"Well, I know this has no reflection on you. You heard what happened at the Casino at Valentine's dance with your son, Carlos?"

"No, what about him? What happened?"

"He tried to grab Dr. Valverde's dick in the bathroom. His sons were so pissed off that they had to teach your son a lesson later in the bathroom. You've got a sissy on your hands, amigo."

Facundo remained seated, motionless, looking straight ahead. He suddenly turned and landed a punch on the man's jaw, knocking him off the barstool and onto the floor. *"Chinga tu madre,"* said Facundo as he threw money on the bar and left.

Chapter 20: The Disinheritance

At home, Blanca prepared a salad in the kitchen and picked up the ringing wall phone.

"Hello?"

"Hello, is this Mrs. Casavantes?" said a man's voice on the other line.

"Yes, this is Blanca."

"This is Mariano Davila, the notary public who works for your husband. I'm so sorry for this call. I must inform you that Mr. Facundo has eliminated your son Carlos from his will. Effective today, he receives nothing upon Mr. Fausto's passing."

"He can't do that to Carlos."

"Ma'am, he can, and he did. This is simply a courtesy call. I had nothing to do with the decision, and there is nothing neither you nor I can do about it."

The notary expected Blanca to hang up the phone; instead, there was a silence, then she said, "Yes, there is. Would you be the one to file a divorce for Fausto?"

"Yes, Ma'am. That would be me."

"Well, advise him that I will sign the divorce for half of everything Facundo has in cash, properties, and land."

"Let me repeat that – just to make sure I heard you correctly. You want fifty percent of everything Mr. Casavantes has? And you will sign the divorce?"

"That's right. Everything split down the middle. And I will not sign anything until I verify that this is so."

"Very well, Ma'am. I'll get back to you."

Later that day, Blanca sat in the living room with Carlos and Bonita. "So, if he's going to play favorites, nothing against you, Bonita, but if that's what he wants to do, then I'll call his bluff. I know the only reason he did this was to force me to agree to a divorce on his terms, but he wasn't counting on my demands. I may have to fight for the fifty percent, but he'll have to go along if he wants to get rid of me."

Carlos knew the reason for his disinheritance was his father's homophobia. Blanca glossed over the facts, shifting the blame onto herself. It was a mother's noble effort to shield her son's feelings. Maybe she suspected he was gay. Mothers always seem to know. If so, Carlos knew she would never want to talk about it. His mother would look the other way, her heart torn between tradition and the love for her only son. She, too, would live in denial and keep the truth at a safe distance.

"Hallelujah, finally!" said Bonita.

Blanca knew Facundo well, "He will give into my demands because he needs his freedom.—and he deserves it, frankly. We will live well, spend carefully. But you, Bonita, can marry for love and not for security or money. You won't end up like girls around here trapped in a loveless and abusive marriage. And Carlos, you can go to any school you want and become whatever you wish. A movie star, I don't care."

"A high school in Los Angeles?" asked Carlos.

"Why not?" replied Blanca, "Let's set up a meeting with Sister Anne. I'm sure she can recommend a good boarding school and help us get you registered."

"I'll call her right now," said Carlos

"Now you see why I was a constant pain on Papa's side? It cost me a few bruises, but I held on until he got tired of me by using what he most wants against him. Your grandmother used to say, 'Don't let anyone know what you really want because they'll use it against you.' Always keep that in mind, children. Always."

Chapter 21: Full-Moons

A few days later, as Carlos and Tulio sat at Cafe Yolanda having a soda, they noticed how people monitored them. They watched people around them talking in hushed whispers. Tulio caught a woman saying something in the ear of a young girl while sitting in a booth across from them. The girl turned to look at them and covered her mouth to giggle. Tulio knew people always stared at him whenever he wore eyeliner and light pink lip gloss. But this time, there was another reason why they were whispering and giggling. He looked back at the girl and stuck out his tongue. The girl looked away in embarrassment.

"I'm going to miss you, Carlos. If I had the money, I would pack up right now to go with you to that boarding school," said Tulio.

"Yeah. We've got to make the most of it. Why don't you come and stay with me over the summer? I'll have to get a summer job. You can look for one too. Who knows, you might be able to stay," said Carlos with hope.

Suddenly, Facundo burst through the café's door and stood in front of Carlos. With a voice loud enough for everyone to hear, he said, "I've signed the divorce papers. I don't want to bump into you in town ever again. I will pay for you to go away and never come back. You hear me?"

Carlos' face flushed with embarrassment, but he remained silent. Facundo looked around to make sure people heard his threats before leaving. "Have I made myself clear?" He asked loudly as he made his way out. The cafe erupted with chatter. Tulio nervously cracked his knuckles. Carlos put cash on the table. "*Vamonos*, Tulio." Tulio followed Carlos out the door, and right before exiting, he flipped a finger at the people in the café.

"Fuck you all," said Tulio.

"Let's go for a ride, Tulio," said Carlos as he got into Blanca's car, "Let's spend our final time together in peace."

They drove in silence. The stillness seemed like an admission of walls crumbling all around them. People were looking at them, talking about them, and avoiding them. Facundo's very public assault on Carlos only made it worse. Carlos did not want to leave town and go to a boarding school. These things were unwanted. He did not want to do it, but he knew that there was no way he could stay here. Today was his last day, and he decided that he would try to make the most of it and give it a fun spin with Tulio, somehow.

They cruised downtown past the curio shops and circled the Plaza Azueta and Our Lady of Guadalupe Church. Then drove to the outskirts of town and parked on the side of the road overlooking Cerro de Gallardo, a landmark hill on the east side of town. They sat on the hood of the car and listened to top hits on the radio tuned into KOMA in Oklahoma City. Tulio brought out a pack of Cool Cigarettes and offered one to Carlos. They lit up, took a puff, and both coughed at the same time, erupting into laughter.

"Why do you suppose we're gay, Tulio?" asked Carlos as he tried to form a smoke-ring in the air, "I mean, nobody taught us about it or abused us. We didn't read about it or see it anywhere." He observed as he stared up at the sky.

"Beats me. I sometimes wonder if every boy is gay. Maybe they just don't get into it?" Tulio pondered out loud.

"No, my cousins are so straight they kind of turn me on," laughed Carlos.

Tulio asked, "You know what Sister Anne would say right about now?"

"Oh, oh. What would she say?"

"She would say, 'This is your cross, and everyone has a cross to bear.' Then I would, of course, open my big mouth and say that if God made me this way, then he made another one just to keep me company and made you."

"Yeah, we're lucky. I don't know what I would do without you. Hey, maybe we're the first homos in the world," said Carlos.

"Nah, someone murdered el Tino, remember?" Tulio recalled. Carlos sobered up and sighed heavily.

A full moon began inching its way behind Cerro de Gallardo and cast an eerie atmosphere on their last evening together. As they listened to "Dream, Dream," Carlos took a short drag of his cigarette. He stared at the yellow moon, "Last time I gazed at the moon was with Jesse. Wherever he might be, we are both under the same moon, looking up at the same stars." Carlos said.

"Are you going to look him up?" Tulio asked.

"Yeah. But I don't know if he still wants to see me. It's scary to think about seeing him again." Carlos shuddered just thinking about it.

He smiled with admiration and looked at Tulio, whose family allowed him to express himself freely--something Carlos never enjoyed due to his father's homophobia. He would miss his best friend: the pretty face, green eyes, creamy white skin, and high cheekbones. Tulio appeared more androgynous with each passing day with his pixie haircut, eyeliner, and gloss. Carlos realized his friend had gone from a newspaper boy to someone magnificent. He suddenly felt a wave of pride of courage for accepting who they really are. Carlos suspected it would be difficult to keep their sexuality a secret. He knew it was all going to come to a head one day. That day had arrived.

"One thing will never change. You and I are brothers for life," said Carlos.

"Till death do us part," said Tulio stepping on his cigarette butt. "And after that, I suspect there may be gay angels in heaven, and we can keep on going," Tulio said with a grin before he started coughing from his cigarette.

Chapter 22: Love Thy Neighbors

The aroma of roasted chiles and toasted cocoa filled the house as Carlos packed his suitcases. Blanca prepared his favorite chicken in mole for lunch. There was no denying he felt great sadness and fear of tomorrow as he packed his suitcase. Carlos looked at his watch and decided to ask Blanca if he could borrow the car to take a final spin around town. "Where are you going?" she asked. "You won't do something silly, will you? Lunch will be ready in about an hour." She said in a worried tone.

"I'm going to pick up some stuff that I left at Tulio's."

Blanca nodded and gave him permission to borrow the car. Carlos drove across the border to Douglas and parked on Tenth Street and C Avenue outside Immaculate Conception Church. At Loretto School, he learned the value of visiting a church for a moment of respite. He walked into the empty church and wondered if he still belonged in a church. As he knelt and started saying the first words of the Lord's prayer, a wave of sadness washed over him, and he began to sob.

Father Charles, who taught him religion classes at Loretto, walked past the main altar and saw Carlos kneeling. The priest quickly picked up that he was in trouble and sat quietly in the pew behind him.

"Carlos, it's okay. This is the house of the Lord. I don't mean to interrupt you. Can I do anything? Do you need to talk?" asked Father Charles.

Carlos sobbed, "Where is God?"

"God is everywhere. God is within you," answered Father Charles.

"No, he's not. Not within me."

"The Lord forgives everything." urged Father Charles.

"Why did he make me like this?" asked Carlos in an upset voice.

"We are all made in the perfect image of Christ."

"I'm not." Carlos sobbed.

Father Charles offered him his handkerchief. "What troubles you, my son?"

The words felt like rubbing a grain of salt on his wound. It reminded him of Facundo's rejection and abandonment. It reminded him that his father had disowned him, and it was hitting him in waves. He trusted Father Charles and said,

"I'm… I'm in love with… another boy. I didn't mean to fall in love with Jesse. Sometimes, I just want to tear my heart out, but I can't. Now my father has disinherited me, and I have to leave home."

Father Charles listened in silence.

"Why is it okay for people to hurt others and wrong for me to love someone?" asked Carlos.

"I understand, Carlos."

"No, you don't understand. How could you? Nobody understands."

"Yes, I do. You are perfect. Just the way you are." Father Charles paused and allowed his first words to calm Carlos down. Then tactfully, almost in a whisper, asked, "Does Jesse love you back?"

"Yes, he loves me, and he told me so over and over, Father, and I believed him. I wanted to believe him so badly. I know it's a sin. I just can't help myself."

Father Charles waited for Carlos to catch his breath. "All love is God's love. There is no wrong love in God's eyes. He made you and now is showing you why. Your love for Jesse is a blessing, Carlos. It is not a sin."

Carlos looked up in disbelief. It was almost as if someone had splashed a bucket of cold water all over him. Wiping his cheeks, he asked, "A blessing? How is it a blessing?"

"Thou shalt love thy neighbor as thyself from the Book of Leviticus. No matter how different they may appear, to love those shunned by others is sacred. God does not make mistakes. He made you as you are with holy intent," Father Charles paused and then said, "This is your mission in life. I am proud of you."

"You mean, my cross, as Sister Anne says? Well, I don't want a cross. I want to love someone and them to love me back. I want to do it now," said Carlos.

"Do you think you are alone? Others like you hide – they are boyfriends, husbands, and fathers. All too afraid of who they are. Most hide it well. Some secretly make the most of it, and others never adapt. A few regrettably take their own lives."

"Husbands and fathers? How could they ever get married?"

"They are unable to face their feelings. Others just went along with society's traditions. Now they have children and even grandchildren and can't turn back." Carlos thought about Dr. Valverde and the Casino bathroom incident. "Pray for them, Carlos, because their life is a living hell," added Father Charles.

"Yes, father," said Carlos.

"There are some who openly admit who they are in the big cities. I pray you to make your way to find these special friends, and they become your extended family," said Father Charles.

"In Los Angeles?" asked Carlos, "There are people like me in L.A.?"

"Yes, lots of them."

Father Charles's words seemed to hit him in the chest, but strangely it did not hurt. He wished Tulio was with them here, listening to words that opened a whole new world for them.

Father Charles closed his eyes in prayer as he said, "Love Jesse. Let him love you. Be good to one another. Respect your body because it is the temple of the Holy Spirit. Most of all, Carlos, do not harm others. Can you promise that?" asked Father Charles.

"Yes, I can promise that."

"Go with my blessing. I absolve you of all your sins in the name of the Father, Son, and the Holy Spirit. Go in peace and sin no more," said Father Charles.

"Amen."

"It gets better. Trust me. It gets much better."

"Yes, father."

Carlos would never forget the serendipitous meeting with Father Charles. And forever wonder if his understanding came from his vast experience or because he was gay himself. He rushed back across the border and stopped at Tulio's home to share the news.

Chapter 23: Farewell

Concerned Blanca might worry about his whereabouts, Carlos rushed home after spending a couple of hours with Tulio. The house was quiet as he tiptoed past her bedroom door. Blanca would close her door and always leave a few inches open. He peeked through the door opening and saw her napping on her chaise lounge. She fell asleep while waiting for him to return to have chicken mole together.

He studied the woman who would readily and always give her life for him. Her hairline was already showing the first signs of gray, and the corner of her eyes slightly wrinkled. But she was still so beautiful to him. To know such unselfish love would leave a mark on his soul forever. Maybe his mother's love is the only true love he would ever get to know. He stood and kept watching her sleep. He was memorizing the moment into his heart so he can recall it later. Blanca opened her eyes. She saw Carlos standing and observing her from afar. She smiled and patted the chair for him to come and sit.

"Was I snoring?" asked Blanca. "Is that why you were staring?" she asked playfully.

Carlos shook his head and sat down beside her. "Talk to me about when I was born. When I was little," asked Carlos.

"The day you were born, the sun and moon stopped. There had never been anyone like you in my life. You were a beautiful baby boy. The doctor thought you would be a girl, so the first weeks you wore pink until I could get baby blue clothes. You never cried, and you let everyone hold you. You were precious, daring, and ahead of your time. The neighbors would ask to borrow you all the time. You would confuse English and Spanish. Then you would come home with unfamiliar words for us. You taught us about Halloween, turkey, and pumpkin pie on Thanksgiving. When your father would pick you up from school, you always convinced him to stop at Dairy Queen and bought an extra cone home for me. I knew you snuck off to the movies, but I said nothing. Why would I?"

"Yeah. I love going to the movies. It seems so long ago when I believed I would be a movie star. I certainly don't any longer," said Carlos with a note of sadness.

Blanca looked out of her bedroom window and said, "You may be miles away from tomorrow on, but you will always live in our hearts. And you keep home in your heart because you have Bonita and me waiting for you with open arms."

"Leaving home breaks my heart," whispered Carlos.

Blanca nodded, "Yes, many years ago, mine broke into pieces. To leave home is to break your own heart. But you heal. Time heals everything."

The five-fifteen train arrived right on time. Trying to keep his feelings inside, Carlos walked with Blanca, Bonita, and Tulio toward the train platform's westbound side. The early evening became gray and overcast, draping the moment with a veil of sadness as they walked in silence. Blanca had her arm around Carlos. Meanwhile, Tulio carried one of the two bags with all of Carlos's worldly possessions. Bonita did not feign self-control. She openly wiped tears from her eyes.

"I will send you my address as soon as I know it," Carlos said to everyone.

"Leave all of this behind," said Blanca, "Leave whatever happened here behind, just like snakes do at the ranch in September. They leave their skin behind, look straight ahead and never look back. Love us, forgive us, wish us the best but leave us behind," said a tearful Blanca.

"Don't worry, Mama. I now know that what happened made me who I am. You were always the best, Mom. When you talk to Papa, tell him I thank him for being my Dad. He will always be my Papa."

Blanca's eyes watered up, and she said something Carlos would forever repeat to himself, "Remember, my son. You don't have to choose, and you don't have to be any one thing. You can be everything. *Adios,* piece of my heart."

Carlos hugged Blanca and Bonita. Tulio produced a brown paper bag with a Hershey's chocolate with almonds, a pack of Cool cigarettes, and a lighter.

"For the trip," said Tulio.

"Gracias, I will write to you, Tulio."

"Right now, I wish I was your boyfriend and not your friend," said Tulio as his eyes teared up and a bit of eyeliner ran down his cheek.

"No, because if we broke up, we would never see each other again. This way, we will be together forever."

"All aboard, Tucson, Yuma, San Diego, and Los Angeles. All aboard!" announced the conductor.

Carlos hugged Tulio tightly as the train whistle cried out to them. Tulio kissed Carlos on the cheek. Carlos smiled and kissed him back, "Farewell, my brother."

He boarded the train and sat in a window seat facing Blanca, Bonita, and Tulio. They watched him from the platform as the train slowly moved. Their heart sank in their chests. They walked along, following Carlos's window. When the train left them behind, Tulio started running to keep up with Carlos.

"Remember that I know the truth," Tulio screamed with all his might, "I know what really happened. I will always remember the truth."

Carlos kept his eyes on Tulio with an open hand placed against the window until Tulio disappeared.

Dear Young Carlos,

The darkest nights bring out the brightest stars. The grief you feel in your heart will disappear once you cease longing for a past that could have been different. It is what it is. Bad things happened, yes. The reason will reveal itself as you learn more about your own life.

Be grateful for the good and the tough times because they made you who you are. Let go of all resentment. It's a useless emotion and keeps you from becoming your best self. Those who wronged you knew no better.

When you get to L.A., let it all go, and let it make you better – feel more, understand more, and love more deeply. Go forth, my friend,

Your Elder Self.

Chapter 24: Last Dance

Nurse Laila sat at elder Carlos's bedside and read his journal. Carlos lay in bed with a heart monitor beeping by his side. He took labored breaths. He tried to monitor her reading and was always curious about her reaction. When she finished reading, she kept her eyes lowered for a few seconds, then she said, "My, what a sad story, Mr. Carlos. This boy had a lot of things happen to him, so young and so alone." Nurse Laila sighed and stood by his bed, "But, it's better now, isn't it? Isn't it better now than back when this boy was around?"

"Yes, it's better. Some people get it, but others never will," answered Carlos.

"I get that. You know, Mr. Carlos, I do. I tell my son, Roy, all the time that just a little mercy stings more than outright hate. Now, how do you know this boy so well? Might this boy be someone I know?" She said, smiling at Carlos.

Carlos put his head back and rested his eyes, "Yes, I'm sure you know him and many, many others like him."

"Yeah. I've seen them around."

"Be nice to them, Laila. They may act out in ways you don't understand. But all they want is to be loved."

"I will. But what happened to Tulio? And Jesse, and the family?" asked Nurse Laila.

"I never returned to Agua Prieta. Blanca and Bonita would come and visit me, but they are all gone now. Mi mama got her divorce and settlement. She never remarried. She just enjoyed her lady friends, played cards, went bowling, learned yoga and how to swim. And, of course, she still went to the church. Papa never remarried either, and eventually, they struck up a friendship that lasted for the rest of their lives. Bonita married Luis and had her big wedding. They didn't have children and, unfortunately, breast cancer took her away soon after mama died."

"And Tulio. Is he still on the border?"

"Tulio came to visit me in L.A. several times. After he graduated from Douglas High School, he met a talented architect while on vacation and now lives with him in Mexico City. He still calls on Sundays."

"And Jesse! Oh, please, tell me. Did you ever find Jesse?"

Carlos smiled. "Jesse wrote me a letter with his phone number in care of Loretto School. Sister Anne forwarded it to the boarding school. I remember shaking when I put a dime in the payphone to call him. When he answered, I knew right away nothing had changed because when I told him where I was, he said, 'Be outside in thirty minutes.'"

"Now, there's a happy moment for you," said Nurse Laila

Carlos smiled and closed his eyes before a serious look came over him, "We had many happy years together until a fateful motorcycle accident claimed his life. That was the darkest day of my life."

"Oh, my! Mr. Carlos, I am sorry. And did you find someone else?"

Carlos's voice broke, and his eyes appeared watery. "Nobody could take Jesse's place. We'll meet up soon up there, you know. Where no one will ever judge us again."

"Okay, Mr. Carlos. It's been a long day, and I think you should get some rest. I'll come back and check on you first thing tomorrow morning. Do you need anything for now?"

"There is something I want," answered Carlos.

"Anything. I will get for you."

"I would like to go dancing. Can you take us dancing?"

"Dancing? Where? You know you're not supposed to leave this place."

"And who's going to snitch, you?"

The following afternoon, Nurse Laila pushed a wheelchair overloaded with sheets down the nursing home's hallway. Underneath the sheets sat Carlos. She slowly wheeled the bundle of sheets past reception and the security guard and onto a side door where Roy, her son, awaited. He rushed Carlos in his wheelchair into the back seat of a waiting car. Nurse Laila ran out of the building and got in the front seat, and they made a fast getaway.

They arrived at the gay area of town around happy hour time and wheeled Carlos down a sidewalk towards The Rendezvous, a popular gay bar on the strip. Carlos smiled and waved at the people walking by. They heard music coming from a storefront and stopped at the front door, "I think this is it, Mom." Roy said while looking up at the neon sign.

"Okay, let's do it," said Nurse Laila

Moments later, Nurse Laila and Roy entered the Rendezvous Club with Carlos in his wheelchair. People were drinking at the bar and milling around. Some watched a drag show on a stage performing the song "We Are Family." Nurse Laila wheeled elder Carlos onto a table next to the dance floor.

She turned to Roy and said, "Wait here for a minute."

She walked up to Lady Divine, the drag queen mistress of ceremonies, and tapped her on the shoulder. They spoke for a couple of minutes, and Lady Divine nodded in agreement. The drag performance ended with applause and whistles.

Lady Divine picked up the mike, "Ladies, ladies, ladies. Give me your attention, please. We have a fabulous guest partying with us today. Now, girls, all I can say is that I hope and pray I get to do this one day. I want you all to dance with Mr. Carlos, a young eighty-five-year-old who came to the party with us today. Now, remember this. If it weren't for people like Mr. Carlos, who broke the ice for us all years ago, I, Lady Divine, would not be up here singing and dancing. I would be in jail. So, let's show him some love. Music, maestro!"

The bar crowd applauded. The D.J. played an oldie, "The Twist" by Chubby Checker. The strobe lights came on, and Nurse Laila wheeled Carlos onto the dance floor. She danced around his wheelchair. Roy, at first, hesitated and then joined in as men and women began forming a dancing circle. They took turns leading Carlos by the hand and turning his wheelchair to the music. Elder Carlos laughed and raised his arms as tears of joy ran down his cheeks.

Chapter 25: Chocolate with Almonds

Later that evening, Carlos lay in his bed and breathed slowly as the heart monitor beeped. Nurse Laila checked the monitor and refilled his water glass. She cut a square from a Hershey chocolate bar and offered it to Carlos.

"Chocolate with almonds. Want a piece, Mr. Carlos?" asked Nurse Laila.

Carlos chewed a tiny corner of chocolate and smiled with his eyes at Nurse Laila.

"You really tore up that dance floor," she said.

"Thank you for being my friend, Laila, and for reading my letters," he whispered.

"You still have more writing to do. You have lots of writing time left."

"I'm moving on soon, Laila. It's okay. It's easier when you have something to look forward to, and I've got lots of friends where I am going."

"You're staying right here with me. The boys at the Rendezvous are expecting us on Friday night," she said with a smile.

"I know this is your job, Laila. But somehow, I believe we cared for each other," said elder Carlos.

"Of course, Mr. Carlos. I love you. You don't know how much I do."

"Life is better when you know somebody loves you, Laila, even when you don't love yourself. Love helps you survive life's unfair choices," said Carlos.

"Get some rest now. I'll come back first thing tomorrow morning," said Nurse Laila with a smile.

"The next letter is in the top drawer waiting for you. Let's wait for tomorrow and read it together."

"Good idea. You should rest for now," said Nurse Laila as she tucked in Carlos's sheets. She checked the heart monitor one last time and tiptoed out of the room.

The following day, Nurse Laila walked down the hallway and turned into room #303 to find Carlos's bed empty and stripped of sheets. She stood at the door surveying the empty room. The head nurse came by when she saw her at the door.

"What happened?" She asked the head nurse even though she knew the answer.

"Yeah, almost as soon as you left last night, he went into cardiac arrest. It was peaceful. He just seemed to close his eyes. I'm sorry. I know you were close." The head nurse patted her shoulder in empathy. "He left a letter in the top drawer addressed to you," said the head nurse.

Nurse Laila sat in the chair that held elder Carlos so many times. She looked around the empty room with pain in her heart. She felt his essence lingering in the air like a faint sweet aroma that embraced her. The room was cleaned out. Everything that belonged to Carlos disappeared so fast – everything except the elm tree outside the window that seemed to droop in mourning. She picked up the letter addressed to her in precise and beautiful penmanship.

The envelope contained a life insurance policy for $100,000 in her name and a note that read, "When things change inside you, things change around you, too. Until we meet again, Carlos." Nurse Laila sobbed quietly.

The bedside phone rang. Nurse Laila remembered it was Sunday and picked up the phone, "Room 303," she said.

"Hola, this is Tulio calling from Mexico City. I want to speak to my friend, Carlos?"

Nurse Laila replied, "Hello, Tulio. This is Nurse Laila. . ." She hesitated, looked down at the letter, and then took a deep breath before relaying the devastating news.

Two days later, Nurse Laila knelt at Carlos's graveside with Roy at her side. A sudden breeze rustled the trees and seemed to caress Nurse Laila's face and hair. Roy helped Nurse Laila to her feet. She opened her purse and brought out a Hershey's chocolate bar. She placed the chocolate on the tombstone, whispering, "With almonds."

~~~~~~